1-ASC-STACKS

T5-CCK-629

Soc
364.125
B651
v

7477521

DISCARD

PKWY. VILLG

Memphis and Shelby
County Public Library and
Information Center

For the Residents
of
Memphis and Shelby County

VOICEPRINTING

Other books by EUGENE B. BLOCK:

VOICEPRINTING

*How the Law Can Read
the Voice of Crime*

by

Eugene B. Block

David McKay Company, Inc.
New York

VOICEPRINTING

COPYRIGHT © 1975 BY EUGENE B. BLOCK

All rights reserved, including the right to reproduce
this book, or parts thereof, in any form, except for
the inclusion of brief quotations in a review.

To Ruth,
with love

Library of Congress Cataloging in Publication Data

Block, Eugene B
  Voiceprinting: how the law can read the voice of crime.

  Includes index.
    1. Voice. 2. Crime and criminals—Identification.
I. Title.
HV8073.5.B58   364.12′5   74-18638
ISBN 0-679-50518-0

Designed by R. R. Duchi

MANUFACTURED IN THE UNITED STATES OF AMERICA

PKWY. VILLG.
7477521
MEMPHIS PUBLIC LIBRARY AND INFORMATION CENTER
SHELBY COUNTY LIBRARIES

PREFACE

In writing this book and in researching the myriad of factual details involved, the author has tried his utmost to proceed with an open mind, limiting himself to accurate facts alone without venturing any personal opinion on the value and admissibility of Voiceprints as legal evidence. On these points the reader may draw his own conclusions.

As the reader will readily perceive, the lines between supporters and serious critics of Voiceprints are sharply drawn. While those upholding the forensic value of this new technique insist that it is scientifically accurate and as reliable as time-accepted fingerprints, others take a decidely opposite view.

Arguments of the latter, in the main, are essentially similar. They contend that the Voiceprint method has not had either the test of time or the approval of the general scientific community, that it is far from reliable, subject to human error, and that in no way can its accuracy be equated with that of fingerprints.

Some men of science even cite still other points in repudiating the value of the technique; men like Michael H.L. Hecker of Stanford Research Institute, who has testified that "a person's fingerprint is formed before birth and never changes, but a person's vocal apparatus is not constant because it changes with age."

And Dr. Robert E. McGlone of the State University of New York at Buffalo was even more blunt and somewhat caustic in discussing the subject in an address at the San Francisco convention of the American Speech and Hearing Association in 1972. Contending that police use of Voiceprints for identifying suspects could involve a 95 percent chance of convicting an innocent person, he concluded with this terse opinion of the Voiceprint method: "It's more a publicity gimmick than a means of proof."

However, since the contentions of Voiceprint critics are essentially the same, the author, to avoid repetition, has not detailed the arguments of defense counsel in each and every case related in this book.

And while he has endeavored to be entirely objective in this presentation, he has been called on frequently by interested people for his own opinion of the value of Voiceprints. In response he has stated his own personal firm belief that the new method is worthy and that ultimately, with probably still more developments, it will be generally accepted as another proven technique in scientific crime detection. In this judgment he shares the views of such authorities as the Michigan State Police, the head of California's Department of Justice, and many others.

ACKNOWLEDGMENTS

With a deep sense of gratitude, the author expresses his profound thanks to the many people in the United States and abroad whose kindly help made this book possible. They include:
Lawrence G. Kersta, Somerville, New Jersey; Lieutenant Ernest W. Nash, Michigan State Police, East Lansing; Michel Mikkelsen, Interpol, St. Cloud, France; Dr. E. P. Martin, Public Prosecutor's Office, Basle, Switzerland; S. F. O'Donnell, Scotland Yard, London, England; Donald L. Baker, Department of Justice, Sacramento, California; Rom W. Powell, First Assistant State Attorney, Orlando, Florida; Michael Loller, Memphis, Tennessee; Police Lieutenant O. D. House, Modesto, California; Byron C. Wells, Indianapolis, Indiana; Alan H. Sheehan, Boston, Massachusetts; E. Kenneth Hayes, Los Angeles, California; Mrs. Florence R. Peskoe, Trenton, New Jersey; Reginald E. Kavanaugh, Highland Park, New Jersey; Jason R. Silverman, Washington, D.C.; William R. Belota, St. Louis, Missouri; Fausto Poza, Stanford Research Center, California; David Davenport, Green Bay, Wisconsin; Ron Hosie, Riverside, California; John F. Evans, Assistant U.S. Attorney, Washington, D.C.; Linda Handershot, Grand Rapids, Michigan; William Urich, San Francisco, California; Bennett H. Brummer, Assistant Public Defender, Miami, Florida; Mrs. Curtis Rodrigs, San Jose, California; Deane L. Bennett, State Forestry Service, Sacramento, California; Joseph C. Doren, Dunellen, New Jersey; Michael P. Kradz, Springfield, Virginia; James Bettinger, Riverside, California; Robert Imerson, Assistant District Attorney, Los Angeles, California; John J. Pribish, Assistant Prosecutor, Middlesex County, New Jersey; Barnes Investigating Agency, Los Angeles, California; Chief of Police Richard Young, Alameda, California; Dr. Ludwig Rosenstein, San Francisco, California; Michael P. Semansky, Deputy

District Attorney, Oakland, California; Ira L. Dubitsky, Chief, Major Crimes Division, Miami, Florida; William Patterson, Fresno, California; Harvey M. Spar, Charleston, South Carolina; Bartley S. Bleuel, Deputy District Attorney, Sacramento, California; Vern Smith, Assistant District Attorney, San Rafael, California.

The author apologizes to others whose names may have been inadvertently omitted.

CONTENTS

x   *Contents*

INTRODUCTION

The author's absorbing interest in Voiceprints, which motivated this book, stems from years of study and close observation of progress in scientific crime detection. While advances have been relatively slow, their objective at every step has been the same—the search for truth. Yet too often the goal has been to prove guilt rather than innocence.

Fortunately, society has long since emerged from the torturous ways of the dark ages—when resort to such superstitions as trial by ordeal was common practice—to the highly technical crime laboratories of today utilizing the latest scientific advances to achieve criminal justice.

My fascination with the subject of crime had an early beginning. It started when I became a police reporter in San Francisco less than a decade after the turn of the century, an assignment that gave me my first insights into the complicated police system and the methods of those in and out of uniform.

It was a time when major importance was given to use of the Bertillon system of identification by physical measurements, a method now regarded as antiquated and used in extremely modified form. Though fingerprinting was common practice at that time, its usage was a far cry from the present highly developed procedures for easy and more thorough indexing; methods that provide identification of finger patterns with lightning speed.

Delving into the history of this procedure, its advances and effectiveness in baffling mysteries, many years later, put the results of my research and personal observations on paper and my relatively recent book, *Fingerprinting*, resulted. The work has since been translated into French and published in Paris.

However, I had barely completed this work when my attention was drawn to sketchy newspaper accounts of the earliest uses of Voiceprints, the most recent forward step in scientific crime detection. They were fascinating reports and I found myself moved to learn everything available about this new technique as a complement to fingerprinting. I was especially interested in learning how Voiceprints could be utilized to vindicate the innocent; their purpose was not only to convict the guilty.

Before long I had contacted the nationally recognized pioneer in Voiceprinting, Lawrence Kersta of Somerville, New Jersey. The result was a personal visit to the latter's laboratories, hours of talk with Kersta, and a continuing correspondence over procedural and technical questions.

Gradually there emerged a desire to present as a book the entire story of Voiceprints, their beginning and their early use by prosecution and defense alike in puzzling cases throughout the country and abroad. Law-enforcement officers, lawyers, and judges in many states and abroad were contacted.

My quest for incisive information naturally led to intimate and prolonged conferences with the two men who had received national attention as the best-known experts in practical Voiceprint use: Dr. Oscar Tosi of Michigan State University and Lieutenant Ernest Nash of the Michigan State Police. Both have appeared as expert witnesses in Voiceprint cases more often than anyone else.

The following chapters then are the result of intensive study and research into this new and highly technical field. Hopefully, they represent my efforts to write the story as it developed, to offer it fairly and with an open mind, with equal and unbiased attention to supporters of the method as well as to the views of its skeptical and more vigorous critics.

The facts are here. The reader may draw his own conclusions.

Eugene B. Block

Part I

A SLOW
UNSTEADY
BEGINNING

I

The Betraying
Voice

Monday night dinner began as a pleasant prelude to what had been planned as a quiet, relaxing evening for August Sunnen and his family in their roomy, comfortably furnished three-story home in Ladue, a popular suburb of St. Louis, Missouri.

Hours later, however, events abruptly took a terrifying turn, and for the next two years the Sunnens lived day and night in haunting fear for their lives until a baffling mystery finally ended with a dramatic and wholly unexpected solution.

Seated around their large dining room table on this warm July 22, 1968, were Sunnen, middle-aged and tall, the highly respected general manager of a large manufacturing company; his attractive wife, Marian; and their four sons, ranging in age from eleven to twenty-one years. It was a group admired in the community as an unusually closely knit family.

After the meal had ended, they moved into the spacious, ornate living room, eager to spend a few leisurely hours together.

The evening passed pleasantly until the ringing of the telephone shortly before ten o'clock brought a sudden interruption. Sunnen hastened to answer. What he heard moments later might have turned many a man to panic, but Sunnen has long been known for his cool headedness and his concern for the welfare and comfort of others.

It was a man's voice addressing the head of the family by name. "I want forty thousand dollars from you," commanded the unseen caller. "Do as I tell you or one of your boys will be killed—maybe even your wife."

Severely shocked, and with his family's safety uppermost in his mind, Sunnen inquired anxiously what he was to do. He was speaking softly, hoping not to alarm the others.

"I mean business," the other interrupted. "Get the money out of the bank; I'll call you later and tell you exactly what to do."

Again Sunnen pressed for further details.

There was no response, and an instant later Sunnen heard a click at the other end of the line.

Sunnen's last words had been overheard by those in the living room. Startled, they rushed to his side, inquiring what could be the matter.

"One minute," Sunnen said comfortingly, and his finger moved hurriedly around the dial to call the police.

He was still relating to his family what had occurred when a radio car with screeching siren came racing toward the house, driving up the medium-sized circular driveway that leads to the garage.

Officers listened and took notes as Sunnen reported what had taken place. He insisted that he could not recognize the voice, though he had tried his best to do so, nor could he imagine why he had fallen victim to an extortionist threatening death.

"Have you had any business troubles with anyone?" a lawman inquired. "Can you think of any reason why you should get such a demand?"

Sunnen merely shrugged his shoulders, stating again that in no way could he account for what had happened. He was questioned closely about the voice itself: Could he recall ever having heard it before? Had it any kind of distinguishing quality?

He replied that he could not possibly recognize the voice; that he had tried to detect anything that might differ from the ordinary tone of a man's voice. It was neither harsh nor loud, he said.

After much further interrogation, a policeman pointed out that obviously there would be a second call, with specific directions for a payment. This, he said, should provide an important clue and enable the police to set a trap.

"We'll install a tape recorder on that telephone in your den to preserve the voice when he calls again," the man added. "Meanwhile the house will be watched by men in plain clothes. Stay close to your phone day and night. Instructions may come at any time. All we can do now is wait."

The men on the scene soon reported the situation to headquarters and in a short time a detail of six officers arrived with instructions to guard the Sunnen home until morning, when they would be relieved by another squad to provide round-the-clock protection and surveillance.

The group was headed by an experienced officer, Fred J. "Pete" Vasel, who had been assigned to assume charge of the case. Vasel, a former St. Louis police supervisor, describes himself as "a hard-nosed cop" and was admirably suited for the job he was tackling. A resourceful, dedicated police officer, he was ready to lead the search for the unidentified extortionist.

With his men he waited through the late night and early morning hours for a second call, but none came. A tape recorder had been attached to the telephone, and Sunnen was told to try to prolong any conversations with the threatening caller in the hope that they might be traced.

Meanwhile at police headquarters records were being searched for the names of known extortionists and blackmailers who had been released from prison within recent years. Detectives fanned out to look for them, but work in this direction was futile.

The second call did not come until the following night, approximately at the same hour as the first. Sunnen listened to the same voice and was informed that he now would receive definite instructions for the payment, which had to be made in large bills wrapped in a package.

"Now, I'll tell you just how I want this done, and be sure no one's in this but you—that is, if you don't want someone in your family to be killed. Listen carefully."

With pencil and paper close-by, Sunnen jotted down these directions:

"Drive in your Lincoln to the Ramada Inn on Natural Bridge Avenue and wait there at the public telephone for a call. I'll tell you then what we'll do from there. And remember, you and no one else. Okay?"

Sunnen threw a hurried glance at Officer Vasel, standing close at his side so that both could listen through the same receiver. The detective nodded his go-ahead sign and the other assured his caller that instructions would be carefully followed. The police now had their first tape recording of the caller's voice.

Vasel, experienced in dealing with extortionists, suggested that Sunnen do as he was directed, but that Vasel would follow at a safe distance behind. "Get your call and I'll take it from there," he said.

Sunnen did as he was told and he did not have long to wait. Snatching the public phone at the first ring, he heard the voice he already had listened to twice before. "You Sunnen?" the man inquired tersely. Assured that it was, he proceeded with further instructions.

"Drive to that gas station around the corner," the speaker began. "There you'll fill up your tank, and be sure to open up all four doors so I'll know there's no one else in the car. Then go over to the garage of the Nantucket Cove Restaurant and I'll meet you there. And, once more, be sure you're alone or you know what'll happen."

These orders were quickly transported by Sunnen to Vasel, who was in hiding very close-by, ready to carry on with his own plans. "From here on in," the detective said in a very low voice, "I'm following his directions instead of you. I'll take your car. You keep out of sight until I'm on my way; then take a cab home."

Vasel had carefully thought out what he wanted to do to trap the man he was after. Driving alone at the wheel of Sunnen's Lincoln, he obeyed instructions implicitly and finally pulled up at the garage of the restaurant to which Sunnen had been told to go. The area appeared to be deserted.

For a time he looked about furtively, suspecting that the stranger might be in hiding, waiting for a safe time to make his appearance. No one came. As tense minutes slipped by, an occasional pedestrian walked leisurely by and the officer's disappointment increased steadily.

After more than an hour he gave up, wondering in his frustration whether his ruse had been detected or the other perhaps had become afraid to continue with his daring plot.

Dejectedly he drove back to the Sunnen residence to await another telephone call. When it came, not long after his arrival, Sunnen listened to an extremely angry and agitated voice. "You tipped off the police," the caller grumbled, "and now I'm really going to get you." That was the end of the conversation.

The family had borne the shock of the earlier calls with amazing courage and self-control, but now realized the increasing danger. The police guard was still posted day and night, but the Sunnens knew that they could not remain under constant guard indefinitely. Sunnen had important matters awaiting him at his office.

His wife couldn't remain at home forever, nor could the boys—James, John, Paul, and Donald—all of them students. They were still on school vacation. However, as time passed and they found themselves obliged to return to classes, they would have to do so under police surveillance. Meanwhile, no one budged from the house. Food and other necessities were ordered by telephone and received by watchful police.

Vasel, remaining almost constantly at the Sunnen residence, worried over the failure of his intended trap, and kept in close touch with his superiors. He was told that little more could be done until a further call was received. The entire St. Louis police department had already been alerted and every man was vigilant. Here and there suspicious-looking characters were being stopped and questioned. A few were taken to headquarters for more intensive investigation, but all to no avail.

More anxious days passed with mounting fear and anxiety, the family uncertain as to what the mysterious caller's revenge might be. In a frenzy he might try to break through the guard about the house. Perhaps he might even shoot from ambush.

Then more phone calls came at shorter intervals, all of them continuing to threaten harm because the police were on the case. In all, there were seven messages—six of them recorded on tape—yet no worthwhile progress had been made in finding even a clue to the man's identity.

News of the family's plight and the fruitless search had become known despite the efforts of the police for secrecy. The story appeared in the widely read *St. Louis Post Dispatch* and in other newspapers in the area. Sympathetic words came from relatives, neighbors, and friends.

Sunnen realized that he could no longer remain away from business. As vice-president and general manager of a large machine tool manufacturing firm, the Sunnen Products Company, many pressing matters awaited his attention and he was anxious to meet with the firm's president, his uncle, Joseph Sunnen. With his usual coolness, he ventured from his still-guarded home, went to his office, and spent most of the day with his colleagues. What his inner thoughts may have been on this first day from home one can only guess.

Frequent conferences with the police continued. While some of the detectives believed that the extortionist probably had given up his demands and his threats, others feared another outbreak. "Until this man is in custody the family and perhaps others remain in danger," one of the investigators asserted. "The only answer is continued vigilance and, of course, continued search."

A year of tension slipped by. Then a second. The calls had long since stopped and the police guard, of necessity, had been withdrawn from the Sunnen residence. The denouement did not come until one morning in July of 1970, almost twenty-four months to the day since the first telephone demand had been received. And the climax was as strange and unexpected as the beginning.

In Sunnen's well-appointed private office a labor negotiating meeting was in progress. During prolonged discussions a trusted employee, thirty-five-year-old Fred L. Crowe, began complaining about his pay and working conditions. He pressed his points, trying his best to be convincing.

Sunnen was listening attentively when suddenly a startling thought went flashing through his mind—Crowe's voice sounded like the one he had heard during the long period of threats and demands!

He asked himself if he could possibly be right. It seemed like a fantastic suspicion; he had listened to Crowe at times since the calls began and had never noticed any similarity. Why now? It was indeed something to think about; anyway there would be a resumption of the labor negotiating session on the following day and Sunnen would have a second opportunity to listen to his employee. Until then he would keep his suspicions to himself. But the suspense was difficult to bear.

Above all, Sunnen wanted to be fair, not only to Crowe but to himself and to the law as well. A man of deep-rooted conscience, he could not bear the thought of accusing an innocent man or even suspecting him, yet as he turned the matter over and over in his mind that night he was haunted by strange thoughts. And no doubt he recalled a much earlier conference with the police when detectives reasoned that the unidentified caller appeared to have singular knowledge of his victim's personal affairs—the make of the car he drove, the number of its doors, and the fact that he was the father of sons. There had even been vague hints of an "inside job."

It was difficult for Sunnen to wait for the following day when he would hear Crowe's voice again. And when that session opened, Sunnen leaned forward in his chair to catch every word that Crowe might speak. The more he listened, the more convinced he became that his original judgment was correct. But, still prodded by his urge for fairness and thoughts of the puzzling two-year interval, he decided on one final move to verify his conclusions. He arranged to have Crowe called before the company's nurse to be questioned privately about an injury he had sustained in a plant accident. During the conversation his voice would be recorded on tape.

That night Sunnen listened to the voice not once but many times, and his judgment was even further bolstered by what he heard. What puzzled him most was why he had not detected the voice similarity long before. He could find no answer, but he realized that the next move was up to him.

Early the following morning he was at police headquarters confiding his suspicions. The officers listened eagerly.

"Of course we'll have to bring this man in for questioning," one of them announced. "He'll deny everything and we have no direct evidence now, but we do have a way of getting it."

Sunnen's expression showed that he did not understand.

"I gather you're not familiar with what we have in mind," the detective ventured. "We'll get Voiceprints and they'll provide us with an accurate answer."

Once more Sunnen looked puzzled.

"Listen to me," said the other. "Let me explain how this new technique works."

And as Sunnen settled comfortably in his chair he listened intently to the officer's explanation of a relatively new invention that produces visible pictures of the human voice. Technically known as spectograms, these pictures, created from a tape recording, make it possible to accurately compare line for line spectogram markings of a suspect's voice with graphs from a tape of another voice, like that from the original menacing telephone call to Sunnen's home.

Sunnen was showing increasing interest.

"Let's talk about the recordings of the messages you got on your phone," the officer resumed. "We have them in our safe. What we have to do now is to have this recorded voice made into spectograms and have them compared with pictures of the voice we all know to be Crowe's—the record your nurse made at the plant."

The officer stated that an expert in the field was available, but he wanted Sunnen to know still more about the process. The technique, he explained, had been developed in recent years by an electronics engineer in the town of Somerville, New Jersey, a man named Lawrence G. Kersta, who had spent more than twenty years in research and experiments at the initial request of the FBI.

Kersta had established the fact that no two human voices are exactly alike, that they differ just as do the fingerprints of every individual, even those of identical twins. To test his conclusions, Kersta had experimented with many thousands of recorded voices and had found no two to be exactly the same.

Sunnen was further told how Kersta had discovered that voice differences, ever so slight and minute, can be detected accurately by using an instrument called a spectograph to transform a voice recorded on magnetic tape into a picture on paper—an actual graphic reproduction of that voice.

"You'll be surprised when I show you one of these spectograms," the speaker went on, "but first let me tell you how Kersta explains it, and I'm going to quote him because I've read it so often. 'Speech,' Kersta says, 'is simply the ability of our vocal tracts to produce recognizable phonetic elements which the ear and brain can translate into words. We speak through our vocal tract—the larynx, the throat cavity, the mouth and the nose. Just as these elements differ in every individual, so consequently do their voices.' "

As the talk continued, Sunnen learned that the use of Voiceprints in recent years had resulted in convictions in cases of extortion, bomb threats, murder, and in situations involving indecent telephone calls. And in other cases, individuals wrongly accused have been vindicated by the same process.

When the conversation finally turned again to the issue at hand, the police suggested that Crowe be brought to headquarters for an interview, but that no actual accusations be made.

Hours later Crowe stood before the officers in a resentful mood, insisting that he was in no way involved in the extortion calls; in fact, he ridiculed Sunnen's suspicions, asking sarcastically how a voice could possibly be recognized after a lapse of two full years.

As he spoke, his manner and some of his statements aroused his listeners. In a few instances he had contradicted himself; in others he appeared too eager to assert his innocence. Finally he was told that he could go; the investigation would be continued.

To make certain that the voice comparison would be made by one of the most experienced experts in the country, the police decided to turn to Detective Lieutenant Ernest W. Nash, head of the Voice Identification Unit of the Michigan State Police in East Lansing, who had studied under Kersta, later playing a leading part in two years of research into the Voiceprint method undertaken at Michigan State University under a grant from the federal Department of Justice. Since then the detective had won wide recognition as an authority in his field.

Nash, after being briefed on the major details of the case, received the tapes taken at Sunnen's home and the one recorded by the company nurse. Running them through his spectograph, he transformed them into spectograms, comparing the patterns line for line. His conclusion, reached after intensive study, was that the two voices, beyond any doubt, were those of the same person.

With this information, regarded as conclusive, St. Louis police began to assemble all of their other material. Crowe's arrest on a charge of attempted extortion followed despite his continued pleas of innocence. More than two years now had passed since the commission of the crime.

Opening of his trial before a jury marked the beginning of a bitter legal fight. The prosecutor, Noel L. Robyn, in his opening statement, declared that Voiceprint identification of Crowe's voice as that of the extortionist provided overwhelming evidence of guilt. This was subsequently corroborated by Nash, who appeared as the state's star witness and explained in detail the methods by which he had reached his conclusion on the voice similarity. Vigorous cross-examination failed to shake him in any way.

As the next witness, Sunnen added his story of the threatening calls and subsequent events.

For the defense, Attorney Samuel Vandover launched into a scathing attack on the scientific evidence, ridiculing Voiceprints and contending that an innocent man was being wrongly accused. Then he injected a political issue, telling the jurors that Sunnen's uncle had been a major financial contributor to the re-election campaign of Prosecutor Eugene McNary. The jury appeared to be unimpressed.

Crowe, then called on to testify in his own behalf, denied his guilt, swearing that at no time did he have any knowledge of what was going on against his employer, except that which was public information.

At last, on January 20, 1972, the trial came to a close. The jurors filed out while many spectators remained in the courtroom eager to learn the accused man's fate. Some questioned how seriously the jurors would regard voice comparisons as a new kind of evidence; others felt certain that Crowe was doomed. However, they did not have long to wait.

Only a few hours later a signal from the jury room advised that a verdict had been reached. After the jurors had returned to their seats in the tense courtroom, their foreman was asked to present the verdict. A tall, angular man rose to his feet, a sheet of paper in his hand, his eyes carefully avoiding the defendant.

"This is our verdict," he announced, and then he read: "We, the jury, find the defendant, Fred L. Crowe, guilty of extortion as charged."

Crowe, his face ashen, swayed and dropped back into his chair.

Two days later he was sentenced to two years in prison, the minimum allowed by statute, a punishment which many believed was far too lenient.

Little more than six months later the law relented. Judge John J. Kelly Jr. of St. Louis County Circuit Court, on July 6 of the same year, ordered a suspension of the balance of Crowe's prison term and granted him probation for six years on condition that he receive such psychiatric care as might be found necessary.

Voiceprints, nevertheless, had demonstrated their role in scientific crime detection.

II

Kersta, The Pioneer

The dramatic solution of the Sunnen mystery, preceded and followed by other cases in scattered parts of the United States and abroad, has resulted in steadily mounting interest in Voiceprints, not only among men of science but among lawyers, judges, and the public as well.

By the spring of 1974 Voiceprint testimony had been accepted by trial courts in thirteen states and for a time in the District of Columbia, until a federal court declared them inadmissible evidence. In fully three states the admissibility of Voiceprint testimony has been supported by higher courts; in others appeals are pending. In some cases Voiceprints have led to convictions; in others to acquittals.

Nevertheless, controversy continues over the method as presently used. Some hail it as a highly significant modern advance in scientific crime detection, comparable in importance to fingerprinting. Others insist that much further research and prolonged testing are needed before the technique is entitled to full acceptance in criminal trials.

As recently as July, 1973, Voiceprints suffered a hard blow in a California trial when a judge rejected the testimony of the two best-known experts on the subject and branded the method as too new and undeveloped to warrant recognition in legal issues at the time.

Ironically, this decision came after Voiceprints had been

accepted in other criminal trials in the same state, and after two appellate courts, also in California, had upheld such evidence. The state attorney general had welcomed the technique as an advance sorely needed to combat increasing crime and violence.

The adverse decision of July, 1973, widely discussed in the press, on radio, and television, was followed by the defense attorney's announcement that he would attempt to reopen some cases resulting in convictions based wholly or partly on Voiceprint evidence. He also filed a $1,100,000 damage suit against the employers of the acquitted man and one of the two experts who testified against him.

Seven months later the same attorneys, defending a university student in a Michigan trial, succeeded again in winning an acquittal for their client when the two top experts disagreed to some extent in their conclusions.

And for a third time, Voiceprints received still another blow in June, 1974, when the United States Circuit Court of Appeals in Washington, D.C., overruled the judgment of the first appellate court of the district and declared Voiceprints to be presently inadmissible as legal evidence. This decision, widely publicized, attracted attention throughout the country in legal and law-enforcement circles.

(These cases will be detailed later in Chapter 24 following a review of typical earlier trials in which Voiceprints have been an important and successful factor.)

The critical court decisions referred to here were a mere slap on the wrist for Voiceprints and spectograph practitioners compared to a scathing article on the subject published in the October 18, 1973, issue of New York's *Village Voice*.

Written by Harry Lee under a San Francisco dateline, it was titled "Your Fingerprints Belong to You, but What About Your Voice?" A more appropriate title, from the author's viewpoint, might have been "Debunking Voiceprints and their Supporters," for the writer, not content with pressing the need for further development, branded the entire method as utterly worthless, ridiculous, and even spurious.

However, he went much further, with serious implications against the ethics of those involved in Voiceprinting and those appearing in court trials. Lieutenant Nash was singled out for bitter criticism, and his ethics were impugned as seriously as his technical performances.

With obvious "tongue-in-cheek," the writer cites in a more or less satirical manner a number of cases involving Voiceprint evidence and he boldly refers to those who have been imprisoned "because of the sound of their voices."

Despite such attacks by Lee and a few less vitriolic writers, supporters of Voiceprints point with assurance and optimism to the equally slow acceptance of other innovations in scientific progress, especially in crime detection. They cite the experience of Alphonse Bertillon of France, who was not only severely ridiculed when he first proposed a system for identifying criminals by physical measurements but threatened with dishonorable discharge from his job. Fingerprints, they say, received the same skeptical reception, for fully ten years had elapsed between the initial opening of Scotland Yard's Fingerprint Identification Bureau and the acceptance by an American court of fingerprints as legal evidence. It has been practically the same with the lie detector.

Voiceprints, its proponents argue, must undergo a similarly gradual approach to general approval in the scientific community. Many arguing with the basic principles of the method believe that technical improvements of the method are sorely needed.

Nevertheless, as Voiceprints continue to command increasing attention in courts and by law-enforcement agencies, public interest in the entire subject focuses not only on its origin and methodology but on the individual who first pioneered the idea and brought about its initial development.

The man credited with these accomplishments is Lawrence G. Kersta of New Jersey, usually referred to as the "inventor" of Voiceprints, though in a strict sense he should be called the original developer of the process.

Actually Kersta followed a somewhat vague idea on which two men in the Bell Telephone Laboratories had done some work many years before with little if any thought of its use in criminalistics. They were merely toying with a theory; its use could be determined later. These two, C. Gray and G. Kopp, abandoned their experiments at the beginning of World War I, and it was not until long afterward that Kersta undertook to make a new beginning in the same field. He did so under unexpected circumstances. The FBI, groping for new scientific ways to fight crime, had turned to Ma Bell for help. The job fell to Kersta, a technician employed by that company.

After fully four years of work, he had developed the technique to a point where he was ready to use it in criminal cases.

In 1966 he resigned his position with Bell to become the president of his own company, Voiceprint Laboratories, Inc., with a plant a few miles from the little town of Somerville, New Jersey. There for seven years he manufactured voice spectographs and other equipment needed for Voiceprinting, trained police to use it, and responded to calls that took him often to the witness chair as an expert witness.

Then, suddenly, business reverses arose. In April, 1973, he was obliged to close down in the face of financial difficulties in the manufacturing arm of the business.

Others, perhaps with more experience in the business world, soon turned covetous eyes on the closed laboratories, with thoughts of resuming the enterprise. No definite plans have been announced, but Kersta now has become scientific advisor to another firm, Base Ten Systems Inc., of Trenton, New Jersey, which recently entered a marketing field for Voiceprint equipment. Kersta also makes himself available as a consultant to others.

For the pioneer, however, abandoning the plant where he had worked so hard was a painful experience. Since childhood his life's interest had been in electronics, and he was proud of what he had achieved at the cost of years of struggling for an education.

He was born in Rochelle Park, New Jersey, on December 22, 1907, and spent his early years on the family's poultry farm, helping with such chores as he could perform when he was not studying at the rural school. Even then his absorbing interest lay in electricity and related fields.

He recalls that at eight years of age, when most of his companions were flying kites or rolling hoops, he built his first radio set and demonstrated that it would work. He was already reading what he could understand about electronics and asking many questions.

After graduation from grammar school, he entered Hackensack High School, where he received his diploma in four years. He had dreamed of going to college to pursue technical studies, but necessary funds were not available.

By good fortune, however, an unexpected opportunity came. The Bell Telephone Laboratories had opened what was called a student assistance course and young Kersta was admitted for a three-year term.

He soon realized that to achieve his ambition of becoming an electrical engineer he must go on for further schooling regardless of the financial problems involved.

When the years of laboratory training ended, he applied for admission to Columbia University, determined to find some way to meet expenses.

On becoming a Columbia student, he soon discovered that his sturdy physique and interest in athletics would serve him well. He was hired as an aide to football coaches, and with the change of seasons he supported himself by waiting on tables or cleaning laboratories.

In 1930, at the age of twenty-three, he received his B.A. degree in electrical engineering, but he still considered himself inadequately prepared to venture into a competitive world. Four years later he was awarded a master's degree in physics. Now twenty-seven years old, he felt ready to put his learning to practical use.

Having proved his mettle in the student group at Bell, he had little difficulty in getting a job in the laboratories at Murray Hill, New Jersey. He continued to serve that company in various capacities for thirty-nine years, until he had developed Voiceprinting and earned a national reputation for·"seeing what others hear," as some writers have characterized his work.

He was not on his new job long when chance shaped his future just as it has in the lives of so many others. He was assigned to be a research scientist in the Speech Research Department of Bell Laboratories, for speech and sound are vital factors in telephonic communication.

"It was on this job," Kersta recalls many years later, "that I first became interested in human voices, due to the fact that the physical speech mechanisms of no two people are exactly alike, just as no two people ever have been found with precisely matching fingerprints. And I was convinced that voice differences in some fashion could be put to effective and practical use."

This was, indeed, a challenging thought, though at the time he had no idea as to how to achieve that purpose. Nor did he dream then that voice variations could be utilized as an ally of the law, or that equipment and techniques would be developed that eventually would speak the words of guilt or innocence for people accused of crime.

The opportunity to explore these potentials came unexpectedly, in a way that set the course of Kersta's life for many years.

It was a call to the Bell people from the FBI in Washington, inquiring whether it ever would be possible to identify voices with the scientific accuracy that exists with time-tested proof in fingerprint comparisons. Someone in high authority in J. Edgar Hoover's offices had conceived the idea that a comparison of human voices—pitch, intensity, frequency, tone, and the like—might prove an effective means of identifying suspects in cases of bomb threats and skyjacking warnings, or perhaps even in tracing foreign spies.

The task of groping for an answer became Kersta's chief assignment because of his work in voice research. He still firmly believes that this interest of the FBI marked the turning point in his career, giving him the opportunity to devote himself to Voiceprinting.

Kersta's first two years of work on this problem were trying, as he spent long days and nights in the laboratory not only applying what he knew about the human voice to the task at hand but experimenting to create the type of intricate equipment that would be required to graph voices.

He was well on his way when he first publicly reported his theory and procedures in a paper titled "Voiceprint Identification" that was read before the Acoustical Society of America at a conference in New York in May, 1962. The paper was received with interest, but there were many skeptics.

The presentation, however, persuaded the editors of *Nature* magazine to invite him to contribute an article on Voiceprints, then a relatively new word to scientists. He opened his paper with this explanation:

"Voiceprint identification is a spectographic method by which people can be identified by their voices. This method may be an important aid in helping law-enforcement authorities to identify criminals who use the telephone to threaten bombings of airlines and public buildings, those who make obscene telephone calls, telephone extortion threats, and kidnappers who make ransom demands. Much like fingerprint identification uses the unique features in the inked impressions of people's fingers, Voiceprint identification uses the unique features in the spectoscopic impressions of people's utterances."

These prophetic words were followed by an optimistic report of his experiments. "In two years of laboratory-controlled experiments," he wrote, "using a relatively small population (123 members), a correct identification score of over 99 percent was achieved using the skills of trained high school panelists . . . over 50,000 identification attempts were made from a library of over 18,000 different Voiceprints."

The article was widely read, and though it presented highly technical details, it left many scientists wholly unconvinced.

Kersta, far from discouraged, continued his work, availing himself of every opportunity to explain the basic scientific and physical principles that were guiding him. "I know," he would say, "that the grounds for the claim of individual voice uniqueness rest with the mechanism of speech. The parts which principally determine Voiceprint uniqueness are the vocal cavities and the articulators. The vocal cavities are resonators which, much like organ pipes, cause energy to be reinforced in specific spectrum areas dependent upon their sizes. The major cavities affecting speech are the throat, nasal, and two oral cavities formed in the mouth by positioning the tongue. The contribution of the vocal cavities to voice uniqueness lies in their size and the manner in which they are coupled. The likelihood of two people having all vocal cavities the same size and coupled identically seems remote. A still greater factor in determining voice uniqueness is the way in which the articulators are manipulated during speech. The articulators include the lips, teeth, tongue, soft palate, and those muscles whose controlled dynamic interplay results in intelligible speech."

In still further explanation he always chose to detail the manner in which speech is acquired in early childhood. "It is well known," he would say, "that intelligible speech is not spontaneously acquired by an infant. It is a studied process of the imitation of those around him who are successfully communicating. The desire to communicate causes the infant to accomplish intelligible speech by literally thousands of trials and errors before achieving success. His success requires that he learn a dynamic complex manipulation of interrelated muscles controlling the movement of several articulators. Now you can see, I hope, why the chances that two individuals would have the same dynamic use patterns for the articulators would be so remote."

Working on this premise, he turned to devising necessary scientific equipment that would make it possible to actually *see* the differences in human voices, however slight these variations might be.

The result was the development of a sound spectrograph which Kersta describes as "an electro-mechanical scientific instrument which has the capabilities of translating acoustical sounds, including speech, into a visual pattern of sounds which we call a spectogram, the Voiceprint."

It was by intensive study of these graphs, with their curiously shaped patterns of lines in strange formation, some lateral and others horizontal, with significant differences in size and shading, that Kersta convinced himself that they could provide accurate means of comparison.

Months of patient testings followed until he was fully

satisfied, as he still is today, that the certainty of accuracy is at least 99.65 percent if tests are made by experts trained to intelligently interpret results.

His work gradually became known, and law-enforcement agencies, federal and local, came to watch his demonstrations and to learn the principles.

Before long he was being consulted on a wide range of problems by the United States Air Force, the Civil Aeronautics Board and other government bodies. It was recognition that softened the blow that came when a committee of the Acoustical Society of America made public a report that "his available results are inadequate to establish the reliability of voice identification by spectograms." Similar criticism came from other scientific groups.

Kersta still recalls the first time that a police department sent to him for help. The appeal came from Connecticut, where a man was being accused of telephoning death threats to a prominent family. Using Voiceprints, Kersta established the suspect's innocence and opened jail doors.

There were more cases in other localities giving Kersta further opportunity to demonstrate his theories and their practical application. He was then approaching the end of nearly four decades in the Bell service; it was time to establish his own company. This he did in April, 1968, when Voiceprint Laboratories Inc., was founded, with Kersta as its president.

Not long afterward a federal government agency unexpectedly marked a significant milestone in Voiceprint progress. It was a grant in excess of $300,000 by the Department of Justice for an intensive study of the worthiness of the Kersta technique.

To achieve that purpose the Michigan State Police joined forces with Michigan State University, and intensive research began under the direction of Dr. Oscar I. Tosi, professor of audiology and speech science at the university, who selected a team of scientists to aid him. One of his top associates was Lieutenant Ernest W. Nash, now head of the Voice Identification Unit of Michigan State Police, and a former student under Kersta. The study continued for fully two years.

Meanwhile Kersta was attracting more and more attention.

He had been summoned to White Plains in New York's
Westchester County where a former New Rochelle policeman
was accused of perjury in denying that he had warned a gambler
of an impending raid.

Kersta, who had compared spectograms of the defendant's
known voice with the unidentified caller, was in grave doubt
whether he would be permitted to testify, but the court
overruled defense objections, holding that it was for the jury to
determine the value of evidence. The courtroom was darkened
and Kersta showed the jury the graphs on which he had based his
conclusion that the accused man was guilty.

Though the jury voted for conviction, there remained
doubt as to the part that Kersta's judgment had played in the
final decision. The trial, however, drew significant comment in
the press. *The New York Times* reported:

"The Voiceprint, a dramatic new identification device, was
introduced at a criminal trial here today in what was believed to
be the first application in a courtroom. Lawyers in several cities
called the development 'revolutionary' and 'pioneering' and they
speculated about the day when Voiceprints could be used as
commonly as fingerprints."

The reporter quoted Samuel Dash, "a criminal law expert
in Washington," as telling the press that "what we've got now is
a whole new issue of law. Maybe we'll get to the day where we'll
keep files of Voiceprints—and just think of their value in
kidnapping or extortion cases."

Others voiced similar enthusiasm over subsequent cases in
which Kersta was participating. In 1970 came the report of the
long Michigan study. It was generally regarded as highly critical
of Kersta's methods.

Though it credited him as the pioneer in the field, the
writers contended that his testing had been inadequate and that
there were serious flaws in his technique.

Tosi's work had involved 34,000 experimental trials of
identification performed by thirty-nine trained examiners. In
essence, the report found that Kersta's criteria were not
sufficiently reliable. It insisted that aural comparisons of voices
should complement matching of spectograms, that the two must

correlate with each other, and that dissimilarities should be considered as well as similarities, something which Tosi's team contended had been ignored by Kersta. There were other points of criticism and considerably more recommendations.

Kersta took the report in stride, pleased by the recognition he had received as the pioneer. And Tosi, who at the outset had been severely critical of Kersta's work, now supported the improved method if carried out as he and his aides had recommended.

Tosi and Nash soon afterward became a team recognized as experts, and calls for their appearance in different cases began to come from many parts of the country. Physically, the two are of contrasting appearance. Nash, now forty-five years of age, is five feet ten inches tall. He is smooth-shaven with sharp features and a pleasing personality. Tosi, slightly older, is stocky and bearded. He looks every inch the college professor. Nash could easily be mistaken for a business executive.

By 1973, the improved technique had been accepted as evidence in trial courts of thirteen states—California, Indiana, Florida, New York, New Jersey, Michigan, Missouri, Minnesota, Massachusetts, Wisconsin, South Carolina, Pennsylvania, and Tennessee, as well as the District of Columbia. Typical cases in most of these areas will be related in subsequent chapters.

As Tosi and Nash continued moving from one trial to another, Kersta was devoting himself in his New Jersey plant largely to the manufacture and sales of spectrograph equipment and to the training of men to use it. Occasionally he was summoned to testify.

It was in the Somerville laboratories that I first met Kersta, a pleasant man of wiry, athletic build, five feet ten inches tall. His hair, carefully combed back, showed signs of graying at the temples. His mustache and small Van Dyke were neatly trimmed. He might well be mistaken for a college professor or the head of a large mercantile establishment.

As he escorted me through his two-story laboratory building, he pointed out the intricate equipment and explained its uses. I was first attracted to a large metal cabinet-like instrument that looked as if it might be a computer. Kersta said that it was a spectograph, the machine that produces spectograms.

About four feet high, three feet wide, and two feet deep, it sat on a table. In addition to numerous knobs and dials, the front panels held two tape reels not unlike a conventional tape recorder. Below the reels was a shiny steel drum four inches in diameter, protruding about eight inches.

Around this drum, I was shown, spectogram paper was held in position by circular springs. To one side of the drum was a metal assembly called a stylus carriage, its purpose being to support a thin metal wire, or stylus, as it moved slowly across the spectogram paper.

Kersta explained that the electrical signal on this stylus makes black marks on the spectogram as the drum revolves in synchronism with a scanner head attached to the same assembly which sweeps repeatedly around a loop of magnetic tape containing what is being analyzed. The entire transition process from tape to paper takes exactly ninety seconds.

Somewhat confused, I asked Kersta to tell me in lay terms how this piece of equipment could transform a recorded voice on tape to a picture on paper.

"Listen carefully," he said, "and I'll try my best. The manner in which this machine transforms recorded words from tape to picture is similar to the way that television pictures are transmitted. In television a complete scene or picture is sent out sixty times each second. Each complete picture, remember, is not sent out all at once but is broken down into tiny elements or dots. The horizontal rows of these dots are the fine lines you see when you look very closely at a television screen. So a complete TV picture, sent in one sixtieth of a second, actually consists of hundreds of fine horizontal lines, each line comprising thousands of tiny dots. The whole process of electrically 'scanning' a scene in the TV camera is done so fast that the human eye sees only a complete picture.

"In the sound spectograph," he went on, "a section, or loop, of magnetic tape about eighteen inches long, containing speech or other sounds to be analyzed, is held round the metal drum that I pointed out. Inside this drum a fine magnetic tape head revolves pressing against the tape loop. To make a complete spectogram, taking about ninety seconds, this head passes over the same tape loop more than four hundred times. As I told you, it's a process akin to the 'scanning' of a scene in the TV camera."

Having thus explained the basic principles of the spectogram operation, Kersta was eager to demonstrate how Voiceprints betray the efforts of popular mimics and other entertainers to imitate the voices of important personalities.

Reaching into a file, he removed a spectogram of the voice of David Frye imitating President Nixon with the words "Let me make this perfectly clear." A voice picture of the same words spoken by the President was placed side by side for comparison. The line patterns were wholly dissimilar.

Kersta's further explanation of the effectiveness of his process in trapping blackmailers, extortionists, and others left an important question unanswered. "If you need a tape recording of an unidentified voice to produce a spectogram for comparison purposes," I inquired, "how is it possible to obtain it in crimes of that character?"

"That's easy to answer," he assured me. "In these days of modern practice, police departments in almost every sizable city use tape machines in their stations to record calls for help, complaints, threatening messages, and the like. That's become standard practice. And in cases such as an extortionist's call to a home, the culprit almost always returns the call and police make certain that the second message is recorded on tape."

Such were Kersta's explanations of his basic principles and techniques, which he utilized in a diversity of cases and which still are being applied with many refinements.

III

Voiceprints
in the
Crucible

New Jersey and California, on opposite sides of the continent, provide significant examples of how very gradually scientific advances like Voiceprints gain legal acceptance. Skepticism must be overcome, and those who support such an innovation are compelled to press tenaciously until they succeed.

This is precisely what occurred in these two states, though in others the admissibility of Voiceprint evidence has been approved with relatively little difficulty.

In New Jersey the first introduction of Voiceprints as evidence in a murder trial met with defeat. Not until five years had elapsed were they finally accepted in another case. In California four years were to pass between the time that an appeal court reversed a conviction based on spectograms and a tribunal of equally high status upheld such testimony.

In both states appellate judges finally agreed that the method pioneered by Kersta had been developed by further study and research to a point where its practical worthiness and reliability had been adequately demonstrated; that Voiceprints therefore deserved a place with fingerprints and other modern tools used in the crime laboratory. Thus did these courts overrule the earlier charge that the technique was too new and untried to justify court acceptance.

This advance in California is of greater significance than elsewhere, perhaps, since Voiceprints have been used in more cases in this state than in any other, California being nationally recognized for its progress in all areas of criminal justice—penology, criminology, rehabilitation, crime prevention, and prison reform generally. The California situation, therefore, deserves detailed attention here.

In this, the Golden State, a jury trial for arson in 1966, resulting in a verdict of guilty, was hailed as the first conviction ever to take place in a civil court in California through the use of Voiceprints. But nearly a year later that judgment was overthrown by an appellate court on the ground that the most recent technique in scientific crime detection had not yet been adequately tested; that only one man, Kersta, had appeared to support its accuracy—and he had vested interest as the pioneer.

Then, four years after the unexpected California high court reversal, another judge in another criminal trial in the same state opened the door to the admission of Voiceprints. This time, however, the appellate court concurred when it was called on to review the case, and a new chapter was written into the criminal history of that state.

The initial case, the one in which a conviction was reversed because of Voiceprints, is an unusual story of old-school police leg-work and common-sense deduction that would do justice to the fertile brain of Sir Arthur Conan Doyle and his more recent successor Erle Stanley Gardner, both of whom solved imaginary crime mysteries by deduction rather than with the help of crime laboratories.

The affair itself had a curious beginning following the devastating and costly riots that began in the Watts district of Los Angeles and spread rapidly into more prosperous quarters of the southern metropolis. What occurred came to be regarded throughout the country as a most critical social rebellion. Many filled the jails, and police were hunting for more of the militant leaders who had set the torch to business establishments and private homes, with resulting losses running into millions. Many were seriously hurt.

Racial tensions continued unabated, and many feared that new and more serious outbreaks might occur. The Watts riots became a national issue, with opinions between liberals and conservatives sharply divided as to the cause. Social scientists came to Los Angeles to study the problem at close range.

At the height of so critical a situation, producers at CBS conceived the idea of doing a TV documentary that would tell the story of the Watts rebellion on a national broadcast with Bill Stout narrating. The title would be: "Watts: Riot or Revolt," and sequences would be built around a carefully selected rioter whose identity would be well concealed so that he might tell his story of revenge without fear of arrest or retaliation. Stout and his colleagues did their work well.

The documentary had its nationwide showing on the evening of December 7, 1965, fully four months after the peak of the pillage. Though it was watched by millions, there might not have been repercussions had its viewers not included the Los Angeles chief of police and an astute, determined assistant district attorney who already had prosecuted several of the rioters and was then preparing for the trials of others. His name was Robert Imerman, and as he watched the television screen he little fancied that he soon would find himself in the midst of an unusual legal struggle, with Voiceprints as one of the key issues.

After numerous scenes of rioting and ruins had flashed across the screen, Imerman found himself staring at a ten-minute sequence that almost shocked him out of his comfortable living room chair. He was looking at a nineteen-year-old black, his back to the camera completely concealing his identity, speaking frankly of the disturbances with a bold recital of the daring role he had played.

Supposedly appearing in the Watts district, he related how he had set fire after fire to demonstrate his hatred of white people. The blazes for which he took responsibility represented a loss of fully half a million dollars, yet he spoke nonchalantly, indicating a definite pride in what he had done.

To Imerman and the many others watching the scene it was apparent that every trick of the television camera had been utilized to protect the speaker's identity. His figure appeared in heavy shadow and was somewhat out of focus.

Before the last of the documentary had appeared, Imerman realized that he must do something about it; that the young culprit must be identified and apprehended and made to pay the penalty for what he so freely admitted having done.

The prosecutor's first step would be to inquire into every circumstance involved in the film production.

He first learned that the documentary had been filmed two months before, and that some time prior the arsonist had been intensely interviewed by the producer and his associates. In the pre-screening talks the young man had spoken much more brazenly than he had when he stood by the camera, spewing hate for all whites and especially for Jews. He had even disclosed how he and members of his gang had made and used destructive "Molotov cocktails," filling bottles with gasoline and inserting rags for fuses that needed only to be lighted. Actually, he had named at least five costly fires which he admitted setting.

"How can we identify this young hoodlum?" Imerman asked himself many times. "There isn't a single clue but the voice that we all heard." He remembered vaguely having read something about experiments with Voiceprints and he wondered whether this new weapon against crime might be of use now.

He had not gone far when he learned that Chief of Police William H. Parker, having witnessed the production, had become so incensed that he immediately had assigned Sergeants Lee Goforth and Eugene James of the Intelligence Unit to investigate, directing that they cooperate closely with Captain Peter Jasich of the Fire Department's arson squad.

The three, soon working with Imerman, requested a rerun of the film, and before it was over they had noted several significant circumstances that might be valuable as initial clues. For one thing, the youth had stated on the program that on a Sunday, August 15, he had been arrested for burglary at the height of a riot in a residential district while he was standing against a chain-link fence that showed clearly on the screen. For another, they observed that the background of one scene disclosed a loan office on 103rd Street in the Watts area. They also noted that the youth was wearing a ring with a stone on the middle finger of his right hand and a Timex wristwatch.

With only these meager clues they launched the intensive and exhausting manhunt that would involve an inch by inch search of every identifiable street shown on the film, an old-style leg-work job that they were determined to press until they achieved the desired result.

The investigators went still further. They arranged to have the film shown to all officers of the two police stations covering Watts, and the police were provided with still photographs of various scenes in the hope of obtaining additional clues.

Days of frustrating plodding ensued with no result until finally the investigators realized that they were following a false trail and would be obliged to retrace their steps. It had become apparent that they had blundered in concluding that a certain scene had been shot on 103rd Street; the street they had seen was a two-way thoroughfare where cars were running in both directions, and 103rd was one-way. They must now broaden the area of their search; perhaps the scene had been filmed on Broadway, Main, or some other street, but its exact location was in doubt.

Their first break came accidentally. Goforth and James were still scouring neighborhoods at random when they were obliged to stop for a red light at Central and Vernon outside of the Watts area. Before them loomed the sign of a loan company that they had seen on the film and believed was located in Watts. This fully convinced them that they had confined their hunt to the wrong quarter.

The sergeants soon decided on a new approach. They began a meticulous search of reports in the police district mentioned by the arsonist as the scene of his August 15 arrest. Hours later they struck pay dirt. It was a record of the arrest of three young men as burglary suspects. One of them, they soon learned, had been rearrested only a few days before their work began when he failed to halt his car for a stop light and he was found to have marijuana cigarettes in his possession. His name was Edward Lee King. He was nineteen years of age and in a general way his physique matched the appearance of the youth seen on the screen, though his features had been carefully obscured.

The young offender's record provided the investigators with still further confidence that they were on the right track. When last arrested their suspect was wearing a Timex wristwatch and a ring inset with a stone.

In spite of this, the officers wanted still further evidence before undertaking a face-to-face confrontation with King. As their next logical step, they moved to the exact spot where King and his companions had been arrested. Their hope was to find the chain-link fence that King had said was close to him when he was captured. It was decided that each would scout five blocks in different directions from that specific location in the hope of finding the fence. They did not have far to go.

By good fortune they soon came upon what they had been looking for. It enclosed the plant of an electrical firm, but unexpectedly a puzzling circumstance developed—the fence appeared to be considerably taller than the one seen on the film. Fearing that they may have blundered, the investigators called on the manager of the firm and learned, to their extreme satisfaction, that the fence recently had been heightened to keep boys from climbing over it. By good fortune, one of the company's employees had seen the film and was positive that he could identify the confessed arsonist if he were to see him again.

Still the officers were not yet ready for a "showdown" talk with King since they were without a full-face front view of the man as he appeared on the film. Their next move, therefore, was to obtain portions of the televised film showing the unidentified speaker and to compare them with police Identification Bureau shots of King.

Despite their handicap, they became convinced that in essential details of physique the two matched better than they had expected. Nevertheless Goforth insisted on going still another step further.

King, it was ascertained, had been a troublesome juvenile, his record starting in the fall of 1960 when he was arrested with several companions for removing flares from a railroad track and using them to smear their names on a high school wall. Other clashes with the law had followed, one for breaking into school lockers, another for trying to slash a boy with a razor blade.

King had admitted to the police that he started smoking marijuana when he was sixteen, that he often consumed as many as four cigarettes a day. This, he explained, helped him to "forget his troubles." His mother, he said, was devoted to church work and he himself followed an Oriental religion.

Sergeant Goforth, in a final ploy to further verify his conclusions, telephoned King's mother. Identifying himself as a writer, he inquired whether her son, Eddie, might be interested in providing some information about the Watts rioting. Mrs. King replied that she was certain he would because, she explained, he had been on a television program directed by a man named Stout.

The time for questioning young King had come. Being unable to furnish bail, he was still in jail for possession of marijuana at the time of his arrest for a traffic violation.

Stout already had been interviewed about the young man he had used in his documentary but, properly asserting his legal rights, he chose to protect his source of information. The officers now were satisfied that he was not needed, for, in their judgment, they had finally put together an airtight case.

King, interviewed in jail, admitted that he was the long-sought individual who had appeared on the television film, stating that he had received $100 for his services. He even boasted that he had been selected from among a number of applicants because of his "negative attitude."

Now Deputy District Attorney Imerman officially entered the case, but he soon found himself confronted by a legal barrier: King's statement, actually a confession, could not be used in court. The United States Supreme Court had recently ruled that in such cases a defendant must be advised of his legal rights and his privilege to have a lawyer appointed for him if he could not afford to engage one.

Imerman realized his precarious legal position. In spite of all the circumstantial evidence, without King's admission of guilt it would be necessary to prove in court that the voice heard over television was actually that of King. Turning over the problem in his mind again and again, and discussing it with his colleagues, the prosecutor finally decided to resort to Voiceprints, of which he knew only little. But he did know of their use in other states; he specifically recalled a news story he had read relating how Kersta had used his invention to solve the cause of a baffling plane disaster.

He telephoned the New Jersey scientist, who expressed his willingness to help in convicting King, now facing a formal charge of arson. To be of assistance, he explained, he would need a section of the television film carrying the accused man's voice and, for comparison, a tape recording of King's voice made while he was in custody.

The latter demand imposed a new problem but it was soon solved. Officers led King into a "bugged" room in the jail and questioned him. In minutes they had a tape recording. No one seemed to question the procedure, the authorities believing that in such a case the end would justify the means.

Imerman then sent the two exemplars by airmail to Kersta. More than a week later Kersta made his report. He asserted that the two voices compared by spectograms were definitely of the same person. The prosecutor now felt confident that all of his problems had been overcome.

Kersta was summoned to Los Angeles by its district attorney, Evelle J. Younger, who since then has been elected California's attorney general. Under Younger's auspices, Kersta was presented at a press conference at which the prosecutor declared emphatically:

"If we're going to win the war against crime we have to develop new weapons—and now we're unveiling one of those new weapons in California."

He was followed by the New Jersey scientist, who explained his techniques, declaring, as he had many times before, that he believed Voiceprints to be as accurate as fingerprints. The press made the most of what had been said.

The county grand jury already had been called into session

and for three full days Kersta appeared as a star witness, beginning with a theoretical explanation of Voiceprints and ending with a point-by-point recital of how his spectograms had convinced him of King's guilt. The result was the return of a four-point indictment charging the accused with arson. That this action was influenced largely by Voiceprint testimony was established months later in the grand jury's annual report.

At the opening of King's trial before a jury, his lawyer, Kenneth Thomas, a 1958 graduate of Ohio State University Law School, launched a bitter attack on the admission of Voiceprint evidence, contending that it would be in violation of the Fifth Amendment to the Constitution, which protects citizens from self-incrimination. He called the "bugging" of the interrogation room to obtain an exemplar of King's voice "deceit."

To this Imerman replied that using the accused man's voice was no different than using his blood or his fingerprints, or accepting identification of a man speaking in a police line-up.

Days of argument on the admissibility of Voiceprints as legal evidence ended when Judge Raymond R. Roberts ruled in favor of the state.

The court's final instructions to the jury were considered fair by both sides. Speaking slowly, with deliberate care in his choice of words, Judge Roberts pointed out that since the evidence was based in large part on Voiceprints, it was for the nine men and three women in the box to each reach a personal opinion on the importance of this new type of testimony. Anyone believing that Voiceprints were not valid, or even seriously doubting their validity, should disregard this evidence in trying to reach a verdict.

Curiously, the jury began its deliberations exactly a year less a day after the nationwide showing of the Watts documentary on television. Closed-room discussions continued for two days, and when a verdict finally was reached the jury found King guilty of arson on one count involving the firing of a pharmacy. To the surprise of everyone he was acquitted of similar charges concerning other burned places of business. Why this distinction was made is still uncertain, though many believe that it was due to conflicts in circumstantial evidence on the charges of which the defendant was acquitted.

When on January 15, 1967, King stood before Judge Roberts to learn his fate, he first heard himself bitterly excoriated, the court branding the defendant's actions as "senseless and malicious." After this long tirade King was committed to state prison for a term of from one to ten years.

Defense Attorney Thomas announced that he had just begun to fight, that he would carry the legal struggle to the United States Supreme Court if necessary. The acceptance of Voiceprints as evidence, he declared, would be the pivotal issue on which his appeal would be based.

His confidence in the outcome of an appeal undoubtedly was supported by a letter written to *The Los Angeles Times* a week later by one of the jurors, Ken Struman, who contradicted published reports with the statement that "the reliability of Voiceprints as a means of positive identification was not accepted by a majority of the King trial jurors . . . there was other evidence more convincing."

Despite the prospect of prolonged litigation, Imerman was well pleased with the verdict, believing that the first and major hurdle had been passed. He pinned his hopes on the likelihood that the defense appeal would fail, but after waiting ten months to learn the outcome, he met with disappointment.

Early in October of the following year the state's District Court of Appeals reversed the judgment of the jury in the lower court. Its opinion was based largely on the contention that Judge Roberts had erred in accepting Kersta's scientific testimony.

The high court's opinion, covering forty-eight pages, termed Kersta's testimony to be primarily responsible for the verdict of guilty. Although other states already had supported Voiceprint evidence, California was not yet ready. The hub of the appellate court's findings was summed up in this key paragraph written by Judge Ralph W. Nutter:

"Kersta's admission that his process is entirely subjective and founded on his opinion alone, without general acceptance within the scientific community, compels us to rule that

Voiceprint identification has not reached a sufficient level of scientific certainty to be accepted as identification evidence in a case where the life and liberty of a defendant may be at stake."

The prosecution, bitterly disappointed, gave serious consideration to an appeal to a higher court but finally decided against such a move.

As Imerman explained long afterward, the trial had come at an early stage of Voiceprint development when only Kersta could qualify as an expert, no one else having engaged in this new field to an extent where his supportive testimony would be acceptable. "We just had to drop our plans for further appeal and accept defeat," the prosecutor told this writer.

Imerman's faith in Voiceprints, however, was not diminished. He believed that some day Voiceprints would stand the test of a high court of appeal. He had little more than four years to wait.

IV

A Reward for Patience

In Los Angeles, Prosecutor Imerman was reaching out for everything he could find to read about Voiceprints and their acceptance in other states. And he waited patiently for the day when they would be admitted as legal evidence in California by a high court of appeal.

Meanwhile another man was working in the same direction. He was Imerman's superior, District Attorney Evelle Younger, who had been thoroughly impressed by Kersta's testimony in the King trial. He had talked to the New Jersey scientist at great length, asking numerous questions to learn all that he could about Voiceprinting and its potentials. The more he heard, the more convinced he became that it was an important and effective addition to the new facilities already used in modern crime detection.

Younger realized that to insist on its use in Los Angeles county would be a futile gesture in view of the appellate court's decision in the King case, but he was a man with vision—and ambition. He also had political hopes, dreaming of the day when he might advance to the position of attorney general of California in which post he would head the state's Department of Justice.

In that event he would have a relatively free hand in introducing the Kersta method throughout the entire state. Even if by then Voiceprints had not won legal acceptance in California, a spectograph made available for the use of each of the state's fifty-eight counties, might at least prove its value in eliminating innocent suspects; perhaps it might even hasten legal acceptance.

Time passed, with Younger maintaining close communication with Kersta and learning of developments in other states where this new kind of evidence was being used effectively. And then, late in 1970, Younger's fondest hopes were realized. He was elected attorney general and assumed that office in January of the following year.

He undertook his new duties with many plans which he knew must be implemented in proper order. In due time he turned his attention to Voiceprints, eager to add it to the facilities at the disposal of the Bureau of Criminal Identification, an adjunct of the state's Department of Justice under his jurisdiction.

On a July morning in 1972 the people of California read an interesting news release from Younger's office. It was a statement in which the attorney general announced, for the first time, that he had acquired for $10,500 a spectograph and other equipment that would make the Voiceprint process available to law-enforcement agencies in every part of the state. He justified this move in a prepared statement in which he expressed full confidence that the apparatus would prove of material help in identifying individuals using the telephone to perpetrate crimes. "Just as fingerprints capture the unique features of fingers," he said, "so the Voiceprint uses the unique features of your utterance for identification."

Calling attention to the effective use of the method in other states in extortion, obscene telephone calls, blackmail and other types of crimes, he proceeded to explain its principles.

"Courts all over the nation," he added, "are coming more and more to accept Voiceprints. Whether it will take five years or twenty-five years to accept the theory that no two voices are the same remains to be seen, but despite legal uncertainties at this time, the possibilities are exciting." And he referred sharply to the skepticism that followed the early use of fingerprints.

To direct the use of this new technique he created a new department to be known as the Voice Identification Unit, under the Department of Justice. As its director Younger appointed a tall, impressive-looking young man who had distinguished himself as the supervisor of latent fingerprints for the state department. His name was Donald Baker and he accepted his new assignment as an intriguing challenge.

So that he might learn the techniques of Voiceprinting, Baker was sent to Somerville, New Jersey, to study the new process at a training center under Kersta himself. He remained several weeks until he had obtained all of the knowledge needed to fulfill his new responsibilities. As he began his training he did not know, however, that even before his return he would be called on to demonstrate what he was learning.

During his absence a sensational jury scandal had arisen and was attracting statewide attention.

In the colorful Southern California city of Riverside, near Los Angeles, a suit for condemnation of property had been abruptly interrupted by charges of jury tampering and attempted bribery. The time was early in April of 1972.

The suit had been brought by Riverside's Metropolitan Water District against a property owner, Nathan Shore, the plaintiff seeking to condemn 640 acres of Shore's land to be used for a contemplated Auld Valley Reservoir. At issue were the Water District's financial offer to the property owner and the amount that he demanded.

The trial was well under way before a jury when a bombshell suddenly exploded. It came from Shore, the defendant, who informed the court that he had received three mysterious telephone calls from a man who, posing as a juror in the case, boldly offered to vote in Shore's favor for a substantial financial consideration.

The property owner's initial disclosure of the offer created a furor, causing a sudden recess in the trial in order to await the outcome of an intensive investigation.

In reporting the amazing situation to the judge, Shore had said that in the first call a man implying that he was a juror in the trial informed Shore "that he and some other people would like to see me make a lot of money on that property."

As the conversation continued, the caller explained that he believed he could influence the jury to agree to pay Shore $1,600 an acre, which meant that the juror would receive a flat sum of $80,000 for his services.

Shore, still pretending to be deeply interested, decided that he would play the secret role of a detective and stall for time. His response was that he would think the matter over.

When a third call came a few days later Shore offered a counterproposition. He suggested the payment of 25 percent of what he would receive from the jury over $1,200 an acre, an offer which would have given the juror $64,000, considerably less than he had wanted. Finally his offer was accepted, but only after the caller had taken care to explain the risk he was taking. "Perhaps you don't realize," he said in a serious tone, "that any one of those eight jurors could blow the whistle." Shore said he understood.

Before that day was over, Shore was in the sheriff's office reporting the results of the game he had been told to play. An investigation already had been started and the finger of suspicion pointed sharply at one juror against whom circumstances seemed to play an accusing role.

This man was questioned, though no hint of an accusation was yet made, and he stoutly denied any knowledge of the bribery plot. In fact, he appeared to be amazed that any of his eleven colleagues would be so daring as to come forward with such an offer.

The sheriff's investigators were far from convinced. They were seriously considering arresting their suspect when someone pointed out that Baker was in New Jersey at the Kersta laboratories and could be counted on to utilize Voiceprints to determine the guilt or innocence of the suspect.

Baker was reached by telephone, advised in detail of the current problem, and informed that tape recordings would be rushed to him by airmail. He was eager to use his newly acquired skills in solving a perplexing problem in his own city.

The sheriff's office already held under lock and key the tape recordings of the caller's voice as taken by Shore during the later telephone conversations. All that was needed now was a recording of the suspected juror's voice for comparison.

Detectives informed this man of the opportunity to clear

himself, explaining that he must voluntarily assume the risk of incriminating himself. "If you choose to take this gamble voluntarily, it's up to you," they said.

"Of course I will—and gladly," the other retorted. "I'm innocent and I've got nothing to hide."

The suspect spoke into a microphone, repeating some of the exact phrases that Shore's anonymous caller had used.

The two tapes were airmailed immediately to Baker, who, despite his training which was nearing a close, asked Kersta to work with him so that there might be no mistake. Comparative spectograms were made and both men recognized at once that the two voices were widely different.

Hours later Baker telephoned the sheriff's office in Riverside with a definite report. "We've finished our work," he announced, "and we have no doubt of our conclusions. You're suspecting the wrong man. These Voiceprints don't match in any respect; they're as different as day and night."

The juror under suspicion naturally was delighted to learn of his vindication, but now the sheriff's office faced a new problem. If the juror they suspected was not their man, who was the guilty juror? The investigation was reopened and through measures that never have been revealed a brand-new suspect came to light.

He was Dewey C. Hodo, a forty-seven-year-old civilian aircraft inspector employed at March Air Force Base. Though he denied his guilt as vigorously as had the other, his manner aroused suspicion, and in discussing the matter he sometimes contradicted himself.

His movements were still being checked when Baker returned home and learned that his expert services were needed again. Before he even could clear his desk of an accumulation of mail, he was asked to put everything aside until he had compared the recordings of the unidentified juror with a new tape of Hodo's voice.

This time Baker came forward with a different report; he was thoroughly convinced that the voices were the same. California now had an expert of its own on home ground.

Hodo was arrested on charges of soliciting a bribe while serving as a juror and soon released on $5,000 bail. What followed was destined to write a new chapter in California's legal history.

The accused man was brought before Municipal Judge Roland Wilson for preliminary hearing. Appearing against him were two key witnesses—Michigan's Voiceprint specialist, Detective Lieutenant Ernest Nash, who had qualified as an expert in the field and was being called from state to state to pass judgment in voice comparisons. The other was Dr. Oscar Tosi of Michigan State University, with equal standing as an authority on Voiceprints and also a staunch supporter of their value.

Both men already had compared tapes of Hodo's voice and of the recordings made by Shore. Already they had reached a definite decision corresponding with that reached earlier by Baker; the voices were identical. The presence of the two Michigan men in court immediately sparked a bitter legal struggle over the testimony that they had come to give.

As the hearing began, Hodo's lawyer, Arthur Lester, announced that he was prepared to challenge the introduction of Voiceprint evidence and he asked the court to bar all such testimony, arguing that Voiceprints had no scientific basis.

Judge Wilson disagreed. He requested the state to proceed with its case; he would rule on the admissibility of the expert testimony later.

Nash, the first witness called, opened with a detailed explanation of the Voiceprint technique, explaining how he had compared the spectograms and reached his final conclusions. He finally made the flat statement that the voice of the man soliciting a bribe from Shore "could not be the voice of any human being excepting the defendant."

Dr. Tosi next took the stand, telling in his own way how he had reached the same opinion. He referred at length to his own intensive studies at the university, telling the court why he was so convinced of the accuracy of Voiceprints.

Barely had he left the witness chair when Lester was on his feet for the defense, bitterly attacking the testimony he had just heard. He referred to Nash's conclusion as "a bootstrap opinion"; in fact he ridiculed the entire Voiceprint theory, calling it inefficient and unsatisfactory.

Nash's statement that he had examined more than 1,750 voices also was criticized, the lawyer insisting that this was an insufficient number on which to support his contentions. Furthermore, he declared that it was highly improper for Nash to look for similarities in spectograms instead of trying to find differences.

Tosi did not escape the lawyer's continued attacks. His statement that the chance of error in voice comparisons was not more than 6 percent was branded as "statistically unacceptable."

Terry Boren, chief trial lawyer in the district attorney's office, was quick to respond. He strongly refuted the contentions of the defense lawyer, arguing that the expert testimony already given should remain in the record. Referring to the disputed 6 percent chance of error, he stated that this applied only to comparisons made under the most pressured conditions.

When he had concluded, the defense attorney renewed his opposition, this time formally moving that the testimony be stricken from the record. Now it was up to Judge Wilson. Reviewing the disputed testimony, he stated that he was ruling in the state's favor because he considered himself "considerably persuaded" by recent federal and state court decisions allowing Voiceprint testimony to be recognized as legal evidence.

Hodo took the stand in his own defense, renewing his plea of innocence, but the court finally held him to answer to the superior court, believing that the evidence was sufficient to justify a jury trial.

The defense, however, was still unwilling to concede defeat in its efforts to free Hodo without a trial in the higher court. It immediately appealed to the district court in the Riverside jurisdiction urging that the holding for trial be set aside on the ground that Voiceprint evidence on which the ruling was based was actually inadmissible and contrary to law.

Through this action Hodo's trial remained in abeyance pending the appellate court ruling, and months passed before it was rendered.

Meanwhile, in Los Angeles, Prosecutor Imerman waited eagerly for the decision, hoping that this time his faith in the Kersta method would be supported. He was not disappointed, though he had to wait long to learn of the final judgment upholding Voiceprints. It did not come until February 22, 1973, months after the appeal had been made.

In legal circles the opinion has been judged a masterpiece of logic and reasoning, the high court referring to the earlier case in Los Angeles with the conclusion that in the intervening four years Voiceprints had met sufficient tests and had been accepted by many reputable scientists.

In the preamble of the decision, summarizing the reasons for reversing the earlier appeal ruling in the Los Angeles King case, the appellate judges now said:

"The Court of Appeal [has] denied the petition [Hodo's appeal] and held that, based on the record of the court below, there was no error in receiving into evidence the testimony of the expert witnesses concerning the results of the Voiceprint tests. The court found that the research of a well-qualified expert witness established that during the four years since the 1968 decision in *People* vs. *King*, holding Voiceprints inadmissible, the technique of Voiceprint identification was supported by scientific and statistical analysis and enjoyed the acceptance of recognized experts in the field."

The decision, written by Justice P. J. Gardner and concurred in by Justices Kerrigan and Kaufman, went on to further analyze the case in its most minute legal details. Portions of the lengthy judgment are worthy of quotation here, reflecting as they do the thorough reasoning of the court. The justices wrote:

"In the preliminary hearing of a juror on charges of promising to render a verdict for a party . . . and offering as a juror to receive a bribe . . . a finding that the technique known as Voiceprint identification was supported by scientific and statistical analysis and enjoyed the acceptance of recognized experts in the field, had sufficient basis, where an expert witness with one doctorate degree in audiology, speech sciences and electronics, and another in engineering and physics, who conducted over 35,000 tests involving over 250 speakers in order to determine the reliability of Voiceprint identification, testified that when a professional Voiceprint examiner has all the time he needs to conduct his tests, is responsible for his decisions, and is able to listen to the voice sampled as well as visually examine the voice spectogram, the Voiceprint method of identification is extremely reliable."

The court then reviewed at length the testimony of both Nash and Tosi, accepting their qualifications, and crediting Dr. Tosi with having refused to approve Voiceprint testimony in a much earlier eastern case until he could acquire sufficient evidence "to prove the validity of the technique."

Looking back on Kersta's appearance as a lone expert witness in the King case, the appellate justices said:

"The foundation for the admissibility of Voiceprint identification in that case [the King trial] was based upon the testimony of Mr. Lawrence Kersta. Mr. Kersta is obviously a pioneer in this field and apparently something of a zealot, whose enthusiasm for his subject carried his opinion beyond the area of acceptance either in the scientific community or in legal circles. Based upon the record before the court in King, we would have no hesitancy in agreeing with the result reached in that case. However, four years have elapsed since King, and further research in the field as related by Dr. Tosi persuades us that the time has come to accept this type of evidence in courts."

The court continued:

"The basis for Mr. Kersta's opinion was certain laboratory tests with 123 employees of the Bell Laboratories. Dr. Tosi conducted over 35,000 tests involving over 250 speakers. At the time of Mr. Kersta's testimony in King, Voiceprint technology was in its preliminary stage of development. Further scientific testing and experiments by Dr. Tosi have established the Voiceprint method of identification and it has now become accepted as a science. As indicated Mr. Kersta was a pioneer. Dr. Tosi has now carefully, scientifically and objectively verified some of Mr. Kersta's preliminary subjective opinions. According to Dr. Tosi, the scientific community has now changed its attitude toward the reliability of Voiceprint methods of identification and there has been an abatement of skepticism among the scientific community as to the reliability of this technique."

Careful attention had been given by the justices to the earlier cases, Cary and King, in which Voiceprint evidence was declared inadmissible. Their comment was that "we hypothesize that, based on the changes in Dr. Tosi's testimony alone, Cary and King would be decided differently today. For this reason we decline to follow these cases."

The decision closed with this terse statement:

"We hold, based on the record of the case below, that there was no error in receiving into evidence the testimony of Lieutenant Nash. Petition denied."

California at last had joined the growing number of states accepting Voiceprints as legal evidence.

That the far-reaching significance of the Hodo decision received due recognition in law-enforcement circles is shown by the attention it was given long afterward in legal and other publications, including daily newspapers.

One illustration is the comment printed months later in "Point of View," the official news report of the district attorney's office of Alameda County in Northern California.

Following a careful review of the facts in the Hodo trial, with due attention to the earlier King appeal, the writer commented:

"This case [Hodo] represents a breakthrough in the area of identification. The court's ruling [the Hodo appeal decision] serves to negate previous California rulings wherein Voiceprint was rejected as inadmissible evidence. These prior rulings were based upon the inability of proponents to demonstrate to the court's satisfaction the degree of reliability [*i.e.,* accuracy needed] to achieve 'scientific acceptance' by those familiar with the workings."

Although both Lieutenant Nash and Dr. Tosi appeared as expert witnesses in the Hodo case, the writer in the district attorney's office chose to pay particular attention to the latter's testimony, perhaps because of his academic standing as head of a university department. In this regard the following comment was made:

"His [Tosi's] background in electronics, audiology, physics, engineering and the speech sciences presented an awesome display of professional expertise. Additionally, the doctor had conducted extensive tests over a five-year period on the principle of Voiceprint. . . . The doctor further testified that all persons who are involved with the science of acoustical spectography accepted Voiceprints as valid means of identification. . . .

"It is interesting to note that the five-year studies conducted by Dr. Tosi have served to substantiate the claims of Mr. Kersta, who testified in the Watts riot case [*People* vs. *King*]. The tests conducted by Kersta apparently were valid but because he was a pioneer in the field, the 'scientific acceptability standard' could not be met [in *People* vs. *King*].

"*The Wall Street Journal* wrote an article on March 20, 1972, discussing Voiceprint with specific reference to Lawrence Kersta (who holds the copyright on the name 'Voiceprint'). The article points out that Dr. Tosi's studies (as reported in 1970) served to confirm the conclusion earlier reached by Mr. Kersta that speakers on Voiceprints could be identified with 99 percent accuracy. Dr. Tosi's studies, of course, have now gone beyond the 99 percent accuracy standard as demonstrated in *Hodo* vs. *Superior Court*.

"Mr. Kersta has gained new fame by being the expert to identify Howard Hughes' voice in the famous January 7, 1972, telephone call where the billionaire industrialist disclaimed his participation with Clifford Irving in an autobiographical venture."

After several delays Hodo's superior court trial finally opened October 10, 1973, nearly eight months after the District Court of Appeals had ruled that the Voiceprint testimony in his preliminary hearing was admissible.

The defense having waived a jury, evidence was heard and weighed by Judge E. Scott Dales, whose ultimate decision was received with surprise and a degree of confusion by many lawyers closely following the case.

Five days were consumed with testimony. Lieutenant Nash,

as in the preliminary hearing, again stated that Voiceprints had established Hodo's guilt beyond doubt. He was followed by four of the defendant's former co-workers, who swore that they had recognized his voice by listening to the tape recordings of the incriminating telephone calls.

Hodo, in his own defense, took the stand and repeated his plea of innocence.

As soon as the defense had rested, Hodo's lawyer, Art Lester, moved that the Voiceprint testimony be declared inadmissible on the ground that the "scientific technique used in evidence in a court of law must be a technique generally accepted by the scientific community."

Lester also referred to the case of Stephen Chapter, some months before in another California court, in which the judge had ruled out all Voiceprint testimony. Prosecuting Attorney Boren replied that despite the Chapter case, the court in deciding Hodo's fate should recognize Voiceprints since they had received the acceptance of a majority of the scientific community.

Judge Dales finally ruled for the defense on the Voiceprint motion, explaining that in his judgment "the test which must be met has not been met here." Evidently he was referring to the specific laboratory tests in the case at issue rather than the Voiceprint method generally. However, he did find Hodo guilty on two felony counts, declaring that he was influenced by the testimony of the co-workers as well as by Hodo's own reading of the disputed phone calls, noting especially that he had recognized "Hodo's very individual manner of speaking and his accent."

Lawyers observing the case quickly pointed out that Judge Dales, in ruling out Voiceprint testimony, had virtually ignored the decision of the appellate court in his own district which, after Hodo's preliminary hearing, had found Voiceprint evidence admissible. His judgment had supported the contrary ruling of the other appellate court in 1968 in another district. Attorneys, referring to this conflict, said it was important to note that the State Supreme Court, the highest in California, had never ruled on the issue.

Their comments, together with those of other judges

elsewhere, were that the appellate court ruling upholding Voiceprints in the Hodo case marked a definite legal acceptance of the method despite Judge Dales' opinion. And they added that since Hodo had been brought to trial on Voiceprint evidence accepted by the appellate court and convicted, the case in effect could be clearly regarded as further legal support of spectogram evidence.

V

Justice
in Reverse

Previous chapters have related cases in which Voiceprints served to convict the guilty. Of equal importance and interest is their role in vindicating the innocent, for Kersta and law-enforcement officers know that they are upholding one of the basic principles of criminal justice in protecting those unjustly accused.

Kersta takes great pride in relating how this modern laboratory tool has sometimes unlocked jail doors. In fact, he cites cases in which he, engaged by the prosecution, found himself obliged to testify that a mistake had been made.

A case in New Jersey in late November, 1968, is a good example. It has important legal significance since some years earlier a court in that state had refused to admit Voiceprint evidence against a man named Cary on trial for murder, the judge holding that spectogram comparisons were too new a technique to be legally acceptable; that their worth had not yet been sufficiently tested.

This time, to the surprise of many leading figures in criminal jurisprudence, the court took a different view: Voiceprints would be acceptable as legal evidence if they were used to prove an accused man to be innocent rather than to establish his guilt. It was an unprecedented ruling.

The man who profited by this decision was John William Krapp, a special policeman, blond and thinly built, with a frame that measured close to six feet six inches. He lived with his wife in the city of Dunellen in New Jersey.

Convicted of making annoying and profane telephone calls to a former fellow-worker, Krapp owes his vindication to Kersta and to Joseph C. Doren, a dedicated and hard-fighting Dunellen lawyer.

According to investigators, hard feelings between Krapp and his accuser, Walter E. Bohn of North Plainfield, had developed two years before the phone calls. Krapp had resented being replaced on his particular job by Bohn when both men were employed by the stationery firm of H. W. Boice in Plainfield. At least this was Bohn's way of accounting for the series of seven disturbing messages—some of them to his home, others to his place of employment.

In the spring of 1966 Krapp left the Boice firm to become a salesman. The calls did not start until February, two years later, and continued until the fall of that year. In the last Bohn was told by the unidentified speaker: "I'm going to kill you right now with a gun."

Doubtlessly the case never would have reached the courts had not Bohn, his patience exhausted, decided after the first few calls to obtain a tape recording of the voice that he was hearing and firmly believed to be that of his former colleague.

As Bohn listened to the tape over and over he became so positive of his identification that he somewhat reluctantly swore to a complaint accusing Krapp of violating a section of the criminal code making it a misdemeanor to use obscene and vulgar language over a telephone.

Krapp appeared with his attorney, Doren, before Judge Augustus S. Drier of the Municipal Court of North Plainfield and vigorously denied the charge despite the sworn testimony of his accuser, who detailed the long series of disturbing messages and his own version of their motivation. He told the court that while at first he had been reluctant to accuse his former co-worker, he finally found himself obliged to take legal action after listening many times to his recordings which, incidentally, had been played for the police.

The court, convinced by this testimony, brushed aside

Krapp's denials and found him guilty. The penalty was a fine as prescribed by law.

Krapp and Attorney Doren announced that they would appeal the decision. This they did with no thought of the unusual action that would follow.

It came after Doren, who had heard much of Voiceprints and their use, began pressing Assistant Prosecutor S. Phillip Klein for an opportunity to have Kersta compare spectograms of Krapp's voice with the recordings that Bohn had made during the telephone calls.

Sensing the fairness of the demand, Klein agreed provided that his superior, Prosecutor Michael B. Imbriani, would authorize the move. The latter had no objection. In the minds of the two lawyers for the state was the realization that they were acting in the highest tradition of their office; that their primary duty was to see justice done whether their side would win or lose.

Now the *state*, rather than the *defense*, called on Kersta for an expert opinion based on Voiceprints. This was an unprecedented move based on a quirk in New Jersey law that permits the use of such scientific evidence to *vindicate* a person, while forbidding it for purposes of conviction—a provision regarded by lawyers as intended to strongly support the basic principle in criminal law that gives the accused the presumption of innocence.

Before asking the appeal court to permit Kersta's testimony, Klein, the prosecutor, wondered whether he might still be refused on some technicality, for he knew of a far earlier ruling in another jurisdiction of the state against Voiceprint evidence. But this, he reasoned, was a different situation and he hoped that he would succeed.

Judge B. Thomas Leahy of the higher court listened to Klein's request with a degree of astonishment as the prosecutor told the court that he considered it the court's duty to hear new evidence that might prove the defendant to be not guilty.

The judge's decision came as an agreeable surprise: he would allow Voiceprint evidence in support of the defense, though he would have been obliged to forbid it if it were presented in further proof of guilt. Both sides were well satisfied.

The next move, before the formal hearing of the appeal and Kersta's testimony, was to obtain an exemplar of Krapp's voice on tape, and this he was happy to provide. He had nothing to lose; the scientific test, he hoped, would bring exoneration. As for Doren, he was assured of his client's ultimate victory, for he was certain of Krapp's innocence.

In a short while Kersta was provided with a recording of the convicted man's voice together with a tape that the accuser had made during one of the abusive calls. Following his customary procedure, the New Jersey scientist put both recordings through his speech spectrograph and obtained lined patterns of the two. These he subjected to close comparison and decided that in no way did they match.

When the appeal hearing opened before Judge Leahy, Kersta, who had been sent for, walked to the witness stand carrying a large briefcase. From it he took a number of spectograms that he had made of the two voice recordings and showed them to the judge, explaining the difference between the two sets of patterns. The variations could be quite readily discerned.

Judge Leahy asked the witness many questions, inquiring with keen interest about the technique involved and the experience that the witness had acquired in his new and specialized field.

"Voiceprints," said Kersta, repeating what he had explained many times before, "are as reliable as fingerprints for identification. They certainly are far more reliable than handwriting comparisons. No one has ever been able to fool the spectrograph, though efforts have been made many times to disguise a voice."

He went on to say that he had worked with many thousand Voiceprints and had compared as many voices. "I have yet to find two voices that provide the same spectograms," he added. "In other words, I have never yet found two voices exactly alike."

The judge then turned to the witness with a pointed question intended to summarize his testimony. "What then, I'll ask you still another time, is your considered opinion of the recordings that you tested in this case?"

"They are the voices of two different people," Kersta replied without hesitation.

Klein then moved for dismissal of the charges.

Apparently Judge Leahy had heard enough. Turning to counsel for both sides he announced that he was now ready to dismiss the charge against the defendant, to rescind the fine, and to allow Krapp to be reimbursed for court costs. He stated that he believed Bohn had acted "in good faith" but that Kersta's long experience with Voiceprints gave validity to his testimony and established reasonable doubt of Krapp's guilt.

Before closing the matter for all time, the judge expressed his opinion that while the Voiceprint technique had been in use for some years, the law had been slow in accepting it, especially since all of this time no serious error had occurred.

The prosecutor nodded in agreement, convinced that he had done his duty in the administration of justice; and the defense, of course, was jubilant. At this point Attorney Doren jumped to his feet exclaiming: "Whatever Mr. Bohn has on tape he's got, but my client didn't do it. Thank God for Mr. Kersta."

To this Klein added: "I too believe Mr. Kersta and feel that the time will come when Voiceprints will be generally accepted."

VI

The Human Guinea Pig

It was inevitable that with the first acceptance of Voiceprints as legal evidence, civil libertarians would cry out against what they considered a violation of the United States Constitution; that protection guaranteed by the Fourth and Fifth Amendments was being denied.

Their protests marked the argument of civil rights against a new type of scientific crime detection, and their claims came at a time when personal liberties were being guarded perhaps as never before. Thin and delicate interpretations of constitutional law were being drawn, and federal courts were being called on for equally fine-point decisions.

As any student of the Constitution knows, the Fourth Amendment provides that "the right of the people to be secure in their persons, houses, papers and effects, against unreasonable searches and seizures shall not be violated. . . ."

The Fifth Amendment, intended basically as a guarantee against self-incrimination in criminal cases, begins with the stipulation that "no person shall be made to answer for a capital or otherwise infamous crime unless on a presentment of indictment of a grand jury." Then, striking directly at its paramount purpose, it continues "nor shall he (any person) be compelled in any criminal case to be witness against himself, nor be deprived of life, liberty or property without due process of law. . . ."

On these guarantees the liberals based their protests against Voiceprints, the lie detector, and like processes aimed at determining guilt. Would a citizen incriminate himself if he obeyed a court order to produce a sample of his voice? Has he the legal right to regard his voice as something private, an untouchable personal possession? Would a court demand for a sample of that voice in a sense be a "seizure"?

Some, pressing the issue still further, began inquiring whether blood and fingerprints were so private and personal as to justify keeping them out of the crime laboratory; in other words, did a demand for a blood test, made to a suspect, violate his constitutional rights against self-incrimination?

The legal test finally began in February, 1971, in a case known as the *United States* vs. *Antonion Dionisio,* a case that would settle the intricate issue for a time, though probably not for all time. Not until January 22, 1973, almost two years later, was a decision rendered.

The case had its beginning in northern Illinois, where a grand jury was in the midst of an intensive investigation of possible violations of federal statutes relating to gambling. Involved in the inquiry were voice recordings that had been obtained by court order. The nature of the suspected violations is not of concern here; pertinent only is the grand jury's desire to obtain voice tests of some twenty individuals whose speech the jurors wished to compare with the recordings in their possession.

Accordingly, the grand jury subpoenaed this score of individuals, directing them to furnish exemplars of their voices.

At the outset each of the group was advised that he was a potential defendant in a criminal prosecution and, as the court of appeals was to recite later in its final decision, "each was asked to examine a transcript of an intercepted conversation, and to go to a nearby office of the United States Attorney to read the transcript, or a portion of it, into a recording device. The witnesses were advised that they would be allowed to have their attorneys present when they read the transcripts."

Dionisio flatly refused, as did the others, and he became the "human guinea pig" in the legal controversy that followed on the contention that the grand jury's order was in direct violation of the two constitutional amendments. The defendants went another step further, arguing that their rights under the Sixth Amendment had been violated by the grand jury in denying them the right to counsel.

Following legal procedure, the government first filed petitions in the United States District Court to compel Dionisio and the other nineteen to furnish voice exemplars to the grand jury. These petitions were supported by the claim that the exemplars were "essential and necessary" to the investigation and that they would "be used solely as a standard of comparison to determine whether or not the witness was the person whose voice had been intercepted."

After a hearing the district judge rejected the constitutional arguments and directed that those involved obey the request of the grand jury. The order was based on the judge's reasoning that voice exemplars, like samples of handwriting or fingerprints, were not "testimonial or communicative evidence" and that therefore an order to produce them would not require any witness to testify against himself. Furthermore, it was the judge's opinion that the Fourth Amendment would not be violated because in legal interpretation the grand jury subpoena did not in itself violate this amendment; that the order to produce the desired exemplars would not require reasonable search and seizure in the context of the amendment. The Sixth Amendment issue also was deemed invalid since the defendants had been advised of their right to counsel.

This, however, failed to satisfy Dionisio, acting not only for himself but for the others as well. Remaining adamant in his refusal to do as the grand jury had directed, he was judged in civil contempt by the district court and ordered into custody until he obeyed the court order or until eighteen months had expired.

Now Dionisio carried the issue to the United States Court of Appeals, which finally settled the controversy by ruling that in this case neither the Fourth nor the Fifth Amendment safeguards had been violated. The high court's reasoning is interesting to follow, since it delves into the authority of grand juries and the rights of individuals.

In support of the grand jury, the judges found that "the grand jury may have been attempting to identify a number of voices on the tapes in evidence or it might have summoned the twenty witnesses in an effort to identify one voice. But, whatever the case, a grand jury's investigation is not fully carried out until every available clue has been run down and all witnesses examined in every proper way to find if a crime has been committed. . . . Neither the order to Dionisio to appear nor the order to make a voice recording was rendered unreasonable by the fact that many others were subjected to the same compulsion. . . . Dionisio's argument was that the grand jury's subsequent directive to make a voice recording was itself an infringement of his rights under the Fourth Amendment. We cannot accept that argument."

Delving deeply into the appellant's contention that a person is entitled to a right of privacy concerning his voice, the court took an opposite view. It responded that "the physical characteristics of a person's voice, its tone and manner, as opposed to the content of a specific conversation, are constantly exposed to the public. Like a man's facial characteristics or handwriting, his voice is repeatedly produced for others to hear. No person can have a reasonable expectation that others will not know the sound of his voice any more than he can reasonably expect that his face will be a mystery to the world."

In support of this conclusion, the court proceeded to quote from the decision of another court in another case:

"Except for the rare recluse who chooses to live his life in complete solitude, in our daily lives we constantly speak and write, and while the content of a communication is entitled to Fourth Amendment protection . . . the underlying identifying characteristics—the constant factor throughout both public and private communications—are open for all to see and hear. There is no basis for constructing a wall of privacy against the grand jury which does not exist in private contacts with strangers. Hence, no intrusion into an individual's privacy results from compelled execution of handwriting or voice exemplars; nothing is being exposed to the grand jury that has not previously been exposed to the public at large."

Citing other cases in which similar issues were raised, the court approached its conclusions with these words:

"The required disclosure of a person's voice is thus further removed from the Fourth Amendment protection that was the intrusion from the body affected by the blood extraction in [the] Schmerber [case] . . . a seizure of voice exemplars does not involve the 'severe though brief intrusion upon cherished personal security.' . . ."

In conclusion, the opinion had this to say about the rights of a grand jury beyond what the judgment already had set forth:

"A grand jury has broad investigative powers to determine whether a crime has been committed and who has committed it. The jurors may act on tips, rumors, evidence presented by the prosecutor or their own personal knowledge. . . . Since Dionisio raised no valid Fourth Amendment claim, there is no more reason to require a preliminary showing of reasonableness here than there would be in the case of any witness who, despite the lack of any constitutional or statutory privilege, declined to answer a question or comply with a grand jury request. Neither the constitution nor our prior cases justify any such interference with grand jury proceedings."

Thus the court gave short shrift to the contention that the grand jury's demand for voice tests violated two constitutional amendments. No doubt civil libertarians will press the issue further in cases that arise in the future.

VII

The Trials That Backfired

The case that ended as a bombshell for Kersta, Tosi, and
Nash, as well as for many other Voiceprint supporters, had its
beginning on February 1, 1972, in the city of San Rafael, the
county seat of scenic, suburban Marin County on the north
shore of San Francisco Bay.

There in early evening a worker in the offices of the Pacific
Telephone and Telegraph Company answered a call and listened
to an obviously disguised voice. The speaker counted from ten to
one, then mimicked the sound of an explosion, and hung up. He
phoned again a little later and this time counted from one to ten
before announcing that a bomb would explode in the telephone
company's office in Mark Drive. His exact words were: "Now to
get down to business. There will be an explosion two nights from
now in your office. You will have to demagnetize all recording
units. This is just a tip. Thank you."

No blast occurred nor was any bomb found despite a careful
and prolonged search.

The calls, however, sparked an intensive investigation by
county authorities aided by the company's security officers, who
were determined to avert further pranks of this sort.

More than a year later came the trial of a suspect and the
unexpected, upsetting decision of a local judge trying the case
without a jury.

An unusual and major factor narrowing the investigation at

the outset was the fact that the threatening call had come to an unlisted number used only by Marin County telephone installers to report and record information about assignments.

This obviously led company officials to suspect one of the eighteen installer-repairmen who regularly used that line to clear assignments, though the same number was available to thousands of employees in the Bay Area.

Reasoning that Voiceprints could solve the mystery, the investigators began by asking the eighteen employees to record their voices on magnetic tape, each repeating the threatening words that had been taped by the company's recording device. This request was met by all of those involved excepting one, who flatly refused. He still insists that he was not told the reason for the request, although company officials say that he was.

The man was Stephen C. Chapter, a pleasant, soft-spoken employee, twenty-eight years of age, happily married and the father of two daughters, six and eight years of age. He had never been in trouble and now he emphatically denied his guilt.

The investigators, still determined to solve their case by Voiceprints, obtained a sample of Chapter's voice without his knowledge by simply tape recording his conversation as he called in routinely to report the completion of a job.

This, with tapes voluntarily furnished by his seventeen co-workers, was sent to Lieutenant Nash in Michigan together with a recording of the bomb-threatening messages. Nash was requested to undertake comparative studies in collaboration with his colleague, Dr. Tosi.

Nash's only response was that he would undertake the assignment on one condition—he would proceed if the Marin authorities would agree to prosecute should Voiceprints convince him of Chapter's guilt. He said he was anxious for still another court test of the technique, especially since this case would be based solely on Voiceprints.

Following customary procedures, Nash compared the spectograms and concluded that the bomb threats had come from Chapter. He emphasized that his final opinion was based on ten points of similarity in the spectograms that he had tested and compared.

On the basis of these findings Chapter was suspended at once from his job without pay and arrested on a felony charge of making a false report of a bomb in a public building. It was an accusation that he still denied. Shortly after, he was fired.

He appeared before Municipal Judge Gary W. Thomas, who, overruling defense objections, permitted both Nash and Dr. Tosi to testify on their Voiceprint comparisons.

Tosi was the first to be called. He explained the technique as a basis for Nash's testimony on the specific issues. After the latter had been heard, Judge Thomas ruled that Chapter must answer to the superior court, as the next highest tribunal in California.

The trial was set for January 29 of the following year, but Dr. Tosi's absence in Europe caused a postponement until July 7.

Meanwhile the case gradually assumed the proportions of a *cause célèbre* in Marin County, with many people rallying to Chapter's defense. Some criticized his discharge from his job, insisting that he was entitled to the presumption of innocence until proven guilty. Journalists wrote columns in pity of the young family now supported only by public welfare; the family's savings were gone and Chapter could not find a job.

Communication Workers Local Union 9404 of San Rafael, of which Chapter was a member, immediately contributed $1,066 toward his defense. The sum grew to more than $5,000, and efforts were made to induce the international union to send additional funds.

Chapter announced publicly that all he wanted was to be vindicated and returned to his $202 a week job. He said that he felt like a guinea pig being used to test "a questionable police technique." "My whole life, my whole future hangs in the balance," he asserted. "Voiceprints seem to be the only evidence they have against me."

His counsel, Robert L. Moran, a young San Francisco lawyer who had appeared for the defense at the preliminary hearing, promised a vigorous courtroom fight which he said would prove Voiceprints "unreliable" and "inadequately developed" at this time.

In press interviews Moran stated that when he first read of Chapter's difficulties, and before he had taken the case, he had suspected that the young man probably was guilty, for he had read of the use of Voiceprints in various trials and presumed that they must be reliable. The preliminary hearing and his own subsequent research had brought about his change of mind. He cited the statement, quoted here in the Preface, made by Dr. Robert E. McGlone that Voiceprints were "more a publicity gimmick than a means of establishing proof."

Then Moran added: "A criminal would have to make his call under ideal laboratory conditions for us to have the remotest chance of identifying him. But if the criminal is making a thirty-second phone call from a noisy bar—the more likely situation—there'd be a ninety-five percent chance of identifying the wrong person."

Attorney Moran knew that he would face a determined opponent in the court trial, for Assistant District Attorney Vernon F. Smith, who had appeared for the state in the earlier hearing, was equally certain of success, relying wholly on the testimony of the two experts. The entire case, he realized, would stand or fall on Voiceprint testimony alone. Contrary to many other Voiceprint cases, there would be no corroborating evidence.

Moran faced his heavy responsibilities as an extremely cautious lawyer. Wishing to be certain in his own mind that he was defending an innocent man, he required Chapter to undergo a lie detector examination. The results verified the accused man's not guilty plea, but Moran wanted still further proof. He insisted on four more similar tests and when they showed the same results, the lawyer turned to another test—sodium amytal, popularly known as "truth serum." At last Moran was completely satisfied.

Now checking through the transcripts of many other cases in which Voiceprints had played an important part, he found that rarely was more than one authority called by the defense to contradict Nash and Tosi, and in some cases there was no rebuttal at all.

Grasping this as perhaps his most vital cue, Moran set out

to summon as many recognized authorities in audiology and related subjects as he could find to contradict the state's experts on the reliability of the method. He ended up with six of his own, only one of whom ever had taken a conspicuous part in Voiceprint cases before.

The prosecutor, forewarned, was unperturbed, confident that he would easily win his case.

The long-delayed trial finally began on Monday, July 9, 1973, before Judge E. Warren McGuire, who had previously announced that the county would allow $2,500 for defense counsel fees and $4,355 for experts because of the defendant's depleted funds. For the same reason a jury would be waived, otherwise the trial might go on for ten days or more.

Despite the wide interest in the case, the ornate mahogany-walled courtroom was sparsely filled when the trial opened. Chapter, neatly dressed and solemn-faced, sat beside his lawyer, who now had been joined by William Urich as associate counsel. Mrs. Chapter took a seat among the few spectators. With them were members of a high school civics class assigned to observe the American trial system.

Nash was the first witness called by Prosecutor Smith. As in all of his appearances, he was first questioned about his qualifications. He told the court that he had received his first training under Kersta in 1967; that he was now president of the International Association of Voice Identification; that he had examined over 3,000 voices and had testified 43 times in 23 states.

He had barely answered the last inquiries when the defense moved to ban all Voiceprint testimony, a motion that the judge denied, explaining that he would first hear all of the experts and then rule on the admissibility of what they said.

Smith, the prosecutor, then played the disputed tapes in open court. Chapter listened attentively, with no show of emotion.

Then Nash related in detail how he had aurally studied all of the tapes, then converted them to spectograms for comparison, and finally concluded that the threatening call had been made by Chapter and "no other human being."

Cross-examination had barely begun when Moran, Chapter's lawyer, played the trump card he had been concealing. He declared that Nash, after examining four additional tapes that the judge had recently ordered taken, had very tentatively, but by no means positively, identified the voice of an assistant district attorney as that of the defendant. He hastened to explain that this had occurred because Chapter had disguised his voice on the tape concerned and was speaking rapidly.

Moran now quickly pressed his advantage. He charged, in a statement to the court, that the state's expert had mistaken the numeral "8" for the letter "E" in a taped version of a work report given by Chapter over a telephone. Then, calling Tosi to the stand, he inquired whether persisting in such a sound comparison should be called "incompetent."

"If they are different, yes," Tosi responded. Moran concealed his elation, believing that Tosi had impeached his own teammate.

With that the trial adjourned for the day, and as spectators left the courtroom and bought their evening papers they learned for the first time of a new development. Moran and Urich, in their client's behalf, had sued the telephone company for $110 million damages, claiming that Chapter's arrest had subjected him to strain and cruelty. Twenty-three others, including Nash, were named as co-defendants.

Early the next morning Moran grasped his opportunity to produce his battery of six scientists to overbalance the two called by the state. The first was Michael H. L. Hecker of Stanford Research Center, a Ph.D. candidate in speech and hearing.

He testified that the range of variability in tones of a person's voice is so wide that it can overlap with the range of variability of another person. He called the term Voiceprint unfortunate, asserting that it erroneously indicates a reliability equal to that of fingerprints which, he explained, are formed before birth and remain constant until death. This was in direct contradiction to the claims of Kersta, Nash, and Tosi who had repeatedly contended that Voiceprints are as reliable as fingerprints.

Next came Dr. Peter Ladefoged, professor of phonetics at the University of California at Los Angeles, who testified that he believed Voiceprint identification can be used as courtroom evidence with reasonable reliability, but he stated that in this view he is in the minority of the scientific community. He said that he had compared the court-ordered tape of Chapter's voice with that of the bomb threat. "It is very unlikely," he declared, "that these are of the same voice."

Reporters felt that the testimony of Dr. Harry Hollien, a University of Florida phonetician, was by far the most convincing in Chapter's behalf. He declared emphatically that he and his team of researchers had detected "two different dialects" in the recordings and he bitterly criticized Nash for his contrary conclusions.

Hollien agreed that Tosi's long research was good technical work, but he insisted that its acceptance as a crime-fighting tool "was like the acceptance of the dolphin talking to people." Then he added: "The fact that Dr. Tosi's research is valid doesn't mean that the methodology of Voiceprints is also valid."

Other defense experts who agreed that the tapes were not of Chapter's voice included Dr. Robert McGlone of State University of New York at Buffalo and Dr. Frank R. Clarke. They also insisted that Voiceprinting was still an undeveloped and unreliable science.

Final arguments by opposing counsel brought the six-day trial to a close, and Judge McGuire announced that he would render his decision on the following Monday morning, first ruling on the admissibility of Voiceprint testimony and then determining the defendant's guilt or innocence.

Early on that morning he rapped for order and began reading his four-page decision. He had not gone far before it became apparent that he was not only tearing apart the prosecution's case but severely criticizing Nash. Probably his most significant conclusion was that the Voiceprint process requires "substantial additional research" before it is accepted by the scientific community, "let alone admissible by the legal community."

After carefully reviewing two earlier California cases, King and Hodo, he directed specific attention to Chapter's trial. Included in his decision were these findings:

"The record before this court clearly indicates:

"Substantial lack of agreement within the scientific community that is concerned with audiology, speech-hearing sciences, and other disciplines relating to the production, transmission, reception, reproduction of speech, speech analysis, speech recognition and acceptance of 'Voiceprints' (spectography). . . .

"That the study undertaken by Dr. Tosi (1968–1970) . . . was a good, necessary scientific laboratory test which met several of the objections to the Kersta study/experiments, was basically devoted to the identification of speech through visual comparisons of spectograms, did not consider nor establish by such testing any application or relation of the technique of field conditions. . . .

"The present level of scientific data and opinion reflects need for substantial additional research in recognized factors affecting both intra-speaker variability and inter-speaker variability . . . before reliability of speaker identification through auditory and spectographic analysis is generally accepted by the scientific community, let alone admissibility by the legal community."

The judge then subjected Nash's testimony to severe criticism. In conclusion, he refused to admit the Nash testimony and found Chapter not guilty. The young defendant beamed and threw his arms around his weeping wife. A few weeks later he returned to his job with the telephone company.

Nash took sharp exception to the decision and vigorously protested as incorrect and unjustified the judge's criticism of his work and testimony. Because of the seriousness of the issue, the following abbreviated summary of the court's words and Nash's later responses to this writer is cited:

COURT: . . . regardless of the issue of admissibility, the opinion of Lt. Nash that the defendant was the speaker of the bomb threat . . . was not reliable . . . due to mistakes and errors in preparation of the spectograms and in making the identification.

NASH: My answer is that it very clearly is not true; the only errors were improper labeling of sounds and words that *were not* utilized in the identification [underscoring Nash's].

COURT: Failure to ascertain the existence of such errors.

NASH: Because the improperly labeled words were not used for the identification it is true that I did not detect the errors prior to trial.

COURT: Demonstrated listening errors in court while under cross-examination.

NASH: The courtroom listening error was not an error. This point illustrates what I have said many times: "There is often a difference between the message being uttered and the sounds of the utterance." Even though the speaker [Chapter] did *not* pronounce the sounds correctly, the power of suggestion would indicate what the message was; in other words, as the judge read and listened, his ears confirmed what his eyes were seeing. At the same time I was not allowed to read the message but rather was allowed to read the improper label done by another person.

COURT: Tentative misidentification of the court-ordered exemplars. . . .

NASH: There was no misidentification of the court-ordered exemplar.

COURT: Failure to maintain adequate records/log during conducting of tests.

NASH: Not true; in fact, this borders on the ridiculous.

Within weeks after the San Rafael decision, Nash's Voiceprint testimony in three other cases in eastern states resulted in convictions. No mention was made of Judge McGuire's adverse ruling in the Chapter trial. In two of these cases appeals were filed.

The second blow dealt to Nash and Voiceprints occurred in a Lansing, Michigan, court in the middle of March, 1974, seven months after the California case.

The Lansing case involved the arrest of twenty-nine-year-old Wayne J. Chaisson, a student at Michigan State, who had a wife and two children. The charge of obtaining $10,000 in securities by false pretense grew out of a highly complicated plot in which mysterious telephone calls from the university campus to a bank and to state police headquarters led to the pickup and delivery of securities that suddenly disappeared and were alleged to have been obtained by the accused.

Suspicion first fell on Chaisson when a police officer who had met him long before, during an investigation, believed he might be involved. He obtained a sample of the suspect's voice, compared it with a recording of the unknown voice calling state police, and believed they were the same.

Comparative tapes were sent to Nash, who reported that they were of the same person. He testified to that effect at Chaisson's preliminary hearing, with the result that the defendant was held for higher court trial.

Chaisson's friends, having heard of attorneys Robert Moran and William Urich, both of San Francisco, and both of whom had had earlier successes in blocking Voiceprinting from court testimony, appealed to them for help. Agreeing to take the case, they soon moved to bar Voiceprint evidence from the trial. Presumably having heard from outside sources that Dr. Tosi might disagree with Nash on the results of the Voiceprint tests in this case, they turned to Tosi and summoned him as a defense witness.

Circuit Court Judge Jack Warren, presiding over the trial without a jury, listened attentively as Tosi testified that in comparing the two voices aurally, he believed that they were the same but that after studying the Voiceprints he had come to reconsider his previous judgment. "I am now less than positive," he asserted from the witness stand. He did admit that he had found "some matches" in spectogram comparisons but insisted again that he was "less than positive" that the voices were identical.

Three other authorities in audiology and phonetics, including Prof. Kenneth Stevens of Massachusetts Institute of Technology, followed each other to the stand, each in his own way asserting that Voiceprints at present did not merit acceptance as legal evidence because the process lacked adequate development.

The prosecutor had heard enough. As courtroom spectators listened in amazement, he moved that the charge against Chaisson be dismissed. Judge Warren readily agreed, and the defendant walked out of court a free man.

This writer learned afterward that the prosecutor's action was not motivated solely by the lack of certainty regarding the Voiceprint results but also by very recent information from the police, who had reconsidered a vital point, undisclosed to this writer, in the evidence.

Later in the day, Nash, in a radio interview, vigorously contradicted the view of the expert witnesses. He asserted firmly that the value of Voiceprints as evidence had been fully established and that he had already been called to testify in a murder case in another city.

VIII

A Major Blow to Voiceprints

It was a complicated legal issue that eventually led to the significant 1974 decision of the United States Circuit Court of Appeals in Washington, D.C., banning Voiceprints as legal evidence in that jurisdiction. The case had its beginning three years before.

The final ruling, because of its somewhat paradoxical nature, attracted nationwide attention, for the high federal court, while repudiating Voiceprints, affirmed the conviction of two defendants on the grounds of other evidence. Earlier a lower federal appeals court had sustained the defendants' conviction in which Voiceprints had played a major part.

To fully understand the uniqueness of the court decision, the case should be related from its start.

At 9:30 on the night of April 9, 1971, an alarming telephone call—"Gimme a Signal Thirteen"—reached the Communications Division of the Metropolitan Police in the nation's capital.

At the other end of the line, Cadet Ulysses Smith recognized the words as a coded emergency call, indicating a police officer in distress. He inquired the location of the trouble and was told that it was at 5010 Grant Street, N.E., in the parking lot of a Safeway Store.

From the outset Smith was suspicious of the message. He had received other such calls while on duty and realized that this time the speaker's manner of voice and choice of words were not exactly in accord with those of a policeman; just what the difference was he could not precisely discern. Accordingly, he stalled for time, pretending that the caller's voice was indistinct because of a poor connection and that he was unsure of the street number. Smith's real purpose was to prolong the conversation as long as possible to provide an adequate recording of the voice on the taping machine attached to the telephone for such situations as this.

Despite his suspicions, however, the officer relayed the emergency call to the police dispatcher, who broadcast it without delay. It was picked up moments later by Sergeant Ronald Wilkins as he was cruising alone close to the reported scene of trouble. Speeding his car, he drove to the address, pulled into the parking lot, and hurried from his machine.

His first steps led him to the rear of the store; he was still uncertain whether a policeman was in difficulty there or perhaps had pursued a burglar some distance away. Seeing no one, he returned to his car and drove to the corner of Fifty-first Street and Grant, where he stopped. There he encountered two men whose actions immediately aroused his suspicions. He thought he recognized them as the pair he had arrested for disorderly conduct about two weeks before, though he could not then recall their names. Not until later were they identified as Albert Raymond and Roland Addison, both of whom were later to play a major role in a courtroom drama.

At the sergeant's approach the two began shouting obscenities as they started running north on Fifty-first Street. Wilkins maneuvered his car in their direction, believing that it would be easy to intercept them. As he did, he definitely recognized Raymond, who apparently was wearing the same clothing as at the time of the previous arrest.

Gaining on the fugitives, Wilkins called to them to halt. His order, however, was ignored, and as they continued their flight he observed them dodging around the side of an apartment building and into a wooded area.

Rather than be trapped alone in the darkness, the officer decided to summon help, but he had scarcely begun to turn his car when both men bolted from the woods, running toward him, Addison about two feet behind his companion.

Raymond was the first to reach the officer's machine. Without a word, he stooped and looked inside, obviously anxious to ascertain if the policeman was alone. He was soon joined by Addison, who also peered into the police car.

It was then that Sergeant Wilkins, sensing serious trouble, reached down to unbuckle his seat belt, intending to jump to the ground and question the pair. He had not yet freed himself when he saw the barrel of a large revolver pointed directly at his face.

He had only time to notice that the weapon was in Raymond's hand. An instant later there was a blinding flash, and the sergeant felt severe, stinging pains in his right hand and left leg. Instinctively, he already had thrown his hands over his face for protection.

Then, split seconds later, he heard two more gunshots and he knew that a third bullet had entered his left arm.

Despite pain and mounting fears for his life, he started his car. Two more shots rang out and a shower of splintered glass fell over his neck and shoulders from the shattered rear window.

With difficulty he succeeded in moving his machine about sixty feet to the corner of Fifty-first and Grant streets. He unbuckled his safety belt, opened the door with his wounded right hand, and succeeded in rolling to the ground, where he took cover near the rear of the car. Then, glancing about quickly, he saw his assailants flee around a corner and disappear.

Now in severe pain, he managed to crawl back to the front seat of the patrol car, pick up his radio, and call to the police dispatcher that he had been shot. He named Albert Raymond as one of the gunmen but he said that he could not recall the name of the second man, though he was certain that he would know it later due to the earlier arrest of the pair.

Fortunately for the wounded sergeant, a number of other officers in radio cars had heard the Signal 13 distress call and had hastened to the Safeway parking lot. One of them, Patrolman Robert Collins, with Officer Arnold Nicholson, had covered the area on foot earlier in the day and had observed Addison and

Raymond loitering about, first close to the parking place and later a few blocks away.

Speeding now on their way in response to the emergency broadcast, Collins and Nicholson heard what they said sounded "like firecrackers." As they maneuvered about, seeking the cause of the trouble, they heard Wilkins' voice over the radio saying that he had been shot and appealing for help.

He was soon found bleeding in his car. While Nicholson remained with him awaiting the arrival of an ambulance, his partner drove on in the hope of apprehending the fugitives. Guided by Wilkins' whispered directions, he drove around and soon came upon one man running toward a Fifty-first Street apartment; a second man was following.

Nicholson pursued them with gun in hand, his finger gripping the trigger. He was chasing the first man, who entered the building, fled to the second floor, and then to the third. In moments, he recognized the man as Addison, whom he had seen by chance at the time of the earlier arrest.

The officer was about to bolt into the building when he heard a warning cry of "sniper" and dashed for cover behind a parked car.

A re-enforcement came minutes afterward in the person of Officer "Buddy" Smallwood, who had responded to the original broadcast for help and soon afterward listened to Wilkins' radio cry after the shooting. The two patrolmen quickly stationed themselves at strategic points and succeeded in capturing both Raymond and Addison without a struggle.

At the hospital Sergeant Wilkins was informed of the arrest. He had been found to be painfully but not critically wounded. He recalled that in the early morning of March 28 he had responded with another officer to a call advising of a serious disturbance on Grant Street, not far from the scene of the later trouble. Arriving there they had observed a crowd gathering and had heard both Addison and Raymond shouting insults at them as they approached. Addison and Raymond were arrested on charges of disorderly conduct. Wilkins' long questioning of them at the station had made it possible for him to identify them so readily after the shooting.

Sergeant Wilkins' two assailants were soon indicted on charges of assaulting him with intent to kill, carrying weapons, and other violations. Plans were made to hasten the trial. Lawyers in the United States Attorney's office were confident that with Wilkins' identification of the pair they had an airtight case, yet for purposes of legal strategy they felt a need to link the accused with the false "13 call" that was regarded as the start of all the trouble; no doubt the call had been intended as a ruse to enable one or both of the defendants to shoot an officer from ambush; that, in fact, it was a conspiracy.

This made it necessary to establish, if at all possible, that the voice first heard by Cadet Smith was that of either Addison or Raymond. There was only one way to determine this; it would require the use of Voiceprints and therefore would require court sanction.

It was now May 14, more than a month after the shooting. Prosecution lawyers appeared in district court requesting both defendants to provide voice samples to be made under the direction of the Metropolitan Police Department within the next five days. Arrangements were made for the two accused men to appear in the offices of the Police Communications Division, under whose supervision the tests would be made. Counsel for the defendants—Jean Dwyer for Raymond and Leonard I. Rosenberg for Addison—were invited to attend. They agreed that one should represent both clients.

When the testing began on May 20, each defendant was requested by Lieutenant Dudley Hunt of the Communications Division to read aloud into a microphone the recorded words spoken by the unidentified person who called the Signal 13 alarm into headquarters.

As soon as this procedure was over, Hunt took the magnetic tapes of the voice samples and mailed them to Lieutenant Ernest Nash of Michigan State Police, together with a recording of the voice of the original caller.

After Nash had completed the customary procedures for spectogram comparisons, he reported, some time later, that he was certain that the voice was that of Raymond. However, to get this accepted as testimony before the court and jury imposed the usual problem of winning the judge's sanction.

The trial opened December 17 and continued for five days. Nash of course appeared as the prosecution's star witness, and the defense counsel immediately launched a strong attack on the admissibility of Voiceprint evidence, arguing, as had lawyers in other cases, that the technique was new and had not yet been accepted by scientists.

In rebuttal, John F. Evans, Assistant United States Attorney, questioned Nash at length concerning his long experience in this field. The witness began by relating his earlier work as an electronics technician for the navy for over four years and his later full-time service in voice identification for the Michigan State Police extending over nearly a five-year period. He was made to tell of his training under Kersta and of his full knowledge of the entire technique.

After he had heard Nash testify, Judge Oliver Gasch ruled that he would admit the disputed evidence. It was one more victory for Voiceprints and their supporters.

Nash then continued with a detailed account of how he had pointed the finger at Raymond as the one who had actually telephoned the police.

His testimony as to the scientific value of Voiceprints was strongly corroborated by Dr. Tosi.

The jury found both defendants guilty as charged. Raymond, regarded as the most culpable, was sentenced to serve concurrent terms not to exceed twenty years; his accomplice was given five years less.

Defense counsel at once filed notice of appeal, and it was apparent that Voiceprint testimony would be the basis of their action.

The higher court's judgment, sustaining the ruling of the lower jurisdiction on the admissibility of Voiceprint evidence and upholding the jury verdict, was an exhaustive document, analyzing every important legal point in the case.

After reviewing the basic facts involved, the judges referred at length to the gradual acceptance of spectograms as legal evidence, citing earlier decisions. Particular attention was given to Dr. Tosi's testimony, the court stating:

"Dr. Tosi's study has substantially changed the opinion expressed by the scientific community as to the reliability of voice spectograms as a means of identifying an unknown voice. A striking example of this can be seen in the case of Dr. Peter Ladefoged, professor of phonetics at UCLA. Dr. Ladefoged stated he believes that spectograms have been established as a reliable method of voice identification and testified in favor of the admission of spectograms in the case at bar."

The appeal judges continued:

"In ruling that the spectographic identification proffered in the case at bar is admissible, this court does not imply that such evidence is mistake-proof or that *any* voice identification should be admitted. Our ruling, based upon the complete record before the court, relying especially on the latest scientific evidence and the expertise of the individual making the identification, is that the spectographic identification of Albert Raymond was clearly reliable enough to be admitted into evidence. The jury, having the benefit of available expert testimony on the subject at trial and fully aware of the facts of the case may give the evidence as little or as much credence as it sees fit.

"The government's motion is, accordingly, granted."

Defense counsel, however, still refused to accept defeat, being determined to continue pressing its attack on the admissibility of Voiceprint evidence. Accordingly, arrangements were soon started to carry the case from the District Court of Appeals to the higher circuit court.

It was this action that reached its final conclusion early in June, 1974, when the circuit court rendered its decision, written by Circuit Judge Carl McGowan. After reviewing various cases in scattered parts of the country pertaining to Voiceprint evidence, the high court stated:

"Appellants challenge the District Court's determination to admit evidence based on spectogram or so-called 'Voiceprint' analysis . . . we hold that the District Court erred in admitting this evidence. However, our examination of this record clearly indicated that the jury's judgment was not substantially swayed by the error."

It was the first time that a federal appeals court had overruled the judgment of a lower federal appeals court on the spectogram issue involved.

Pointedly, the ruling continued:

". . . while portions of the record suggest that spectogram analysis may become a useful tool for the resolution of questions of criminal liability, it is equally clear that techniques of speaker identification by spectogram comparison have not attained the general acceptance of the scientific community to the degree required in this jurisdiction. . . .

"Whatever its promise may be for the future, Voiceprint identification is not now sufficiently accepted by the scientific community as a whole to form a basis for a jury's determination of guilt or innocence. We hold that the District Court erred in determining that this type of evidence is admissible in criminal trials."

(The decision, naturally, applies only to the District of Columbia.)

The high court then turned to other evidence presented by the prosecution, such as the identification of the accused by police officers, and concluded that this and other physical evidence justified a conviction without consideration of Voiceprints.

In sum, the circuit court concluded its decision with these words:

". . . we find the record of guilt in this case to be so overwhelming as to make remand unnecessary.

"The convictions in both appeals are affirmed."

IX

Science
Marches On

In the late sixties when Lawrence Kersta announced the development of Voiceprints, he probably believed that for years they would represent the very latest innovation in scientific crime detection. If he did, he had not reckoned with the rapid progress of science in every field.

By a curious and interesting coincidence, Voiceprints were followed within the same decade by another dramatic forward step, the Psychological Stress Evaluator, a modernization of the conventional lie detector, or polygraph.

This advance, now in practical use in various parts of the country, is the product of three men who pooled the experience they had gained in World War II when they were serving in intelligence and counterespionage activities. They are Allan Bell Jr., Charles McQuiston, and William Ford, now operating under the name of Dektor Counterintelligence and Security, Inc., with national headquarters in Springfield, Virginia.

Their process differs markedly from Voiceprints in purpose as well as in equipment, though the human voice is the basic medium utilized in both. In the case of the Psychological Stress Evaluator, now better known as PSE, its creators have devised both techniques and apparatus to detect lies in a way that they and many others believe to be more accurate and effective than the polygraph, the so-called lie detector. They say that PSE already is being used by more than 150 law-enforcement agencies and commercial organizations in scattered parts of the United States. What the future holds for it, only time and continued tests will tell.

Essentially, the difference between Voiceprints and PSE is that the former functions through a comparison of voices to identify an unknown with a known; the latter tests a specimen of a single known voice to determine whether the speaker is telling truth or lies. It analyzes the voice to detect evidences of the stress that betrays falsehood and concealment.

In essence, PSE comes as the latest method in the centuries-old quest for effective ways to put the brand of "liar" on those who do not speak the truth. The search had its beginning in antiquity.

How far that search has progressed was demonstrated in 1973, when the brutal bathtub murder of a woman in California was solved partly through the use of PSE, which also is said to have been applied in an experimental and unofficial way to the voices of Watergate witnesses before the Select Senate Committee. But more of this later.

Perhaps the inventors of PSE had in mind the words of Dr. Hans Gross, a former Austrian magistrate, known as "the father of criminalistics," when he wrote in the middle of the nineteenth century: "In a certain sense, a large part of the criminalist's work is nothing more than a battle against lies. He has to discover the truth and must fight the opposite. He meets the opposite at every step."

But the problem of separating lies from truth was recognized ages before Gross, even in pagan times, when weird and superstitious practices, often involving pain and torture, were followed as a means of detecting falsehoods.

In tribal days, for example, a person suspected of withholding the truth often was made to seize with his hand a white-hot piece of metal and to carry it for nine feet. There the hand was bandaged and if, after three days, it showed signs of scars, the unfortunate person was publicly declared a liar and punished in a variety of ways.

Early Orientals followed a different method. They fed a mouthful of rice to a suspect who was then deemed guilty of telling untruths if he could not spit out all of the rice, the theory being that a guilty conscience slowed or completely stopped the flow of saliva.

And, of course, there is the story of King Solomon, who found himself obliged to determine which of two women was telling the truth in claiming a child as her own. By ordering the child to be cut in two, the wise ruler concluded rightly that the truthful woman would be the one who willingly relinquished her claim in order to save the child's life.

Early history abounds with strange accounts, but it was not until the early part of the nineteenth century that Cesare Lombroso pioneered in experiments with heart beats as a means of detecting lying, an interesting forerunner of the lie detector— and now of the Psychological Stress Evaluator.

Sure of the accuracy of his theory, Lombroso, in the many books he wrote between 1863 and 1909, recorded numbers of effective tests, including one concerning a notorious horse thief whose heart-beat reactions proved him to be guilty of one crime and innocent of another. It was on Lombroso's early heart-beat principle that later criminalists based their developments of the complicated lie-detecting machine, but progress was slow, as other methods and theories were tried and abandoned.

While some experts were continuing to experiment with Lombroso's heart-beat theory, others, like Dr. R. E. House of Texas, turned in different directions in the 1920s. It was he who held the attention of professional meetings with discourses on the use of "truth serum"—scopolamine—with which he was making many tests. He was convinced that a subject under the influence of the drug would lose all inhibitions and only speak the truth. Unfortunately, House died in the midst of his work. Shortly before his demise he wrote that "the day is not far distant when science will not only prevent 75 percent of crime but convict those who are guilty."

Then a new theory for the same purpose evolved. Its sponsors called it the "association test." A person suspected of a crime was made to listen to the reading of some one hundred words well prepared in advance. Some words were wholly unrelated to the crime, but carefully interspersed were some that bore directly on the offense. The subject was required to respond to each word with the first idea entering his mind an instant after the word was spoken. Theoretically he would incriminate himself by his answer—or unconscious hesitation—when hearing a word associated directly or indirectly with the crime.

"Association tests" were finally dropped. Meanwhile Harvard Professor Hugo Munsterberg continued to work toward the production of the lie detector, an instrument that would measure heart beats, respiration, and blood pressure under emotional stress.

Not until about 1920 did serious developments come in this direction. It was then that August Vollmer, at that time chief of the so-called scientific police force of Berkeley, California, and later a professor of criminology at the University of California, put the Munsterberg idea into practical use. Working first with one of his own officers, John A. Larson (later to become assistant state criminologist of Illinois), and afterward working with Leonardo Keeler (a former Los Angeles policeman), Vollmer succeeded in fashioning a forerunner of today's often-used lie detector, a complicated piece of equipment that records graphs on paper with up and down lines like a seismograph pattern, showing changes in heart beats, blood pressure, and respiration through the use of straps around the subject's body.

Their early experiments drew criticism in certain quarters, with some contending that most subjects of tests, fully conscious of the seriousness of what they were undergoing, would naturally show nervous and emotional reactions, thus resulting in false and misleading graphs.

However, Vollmer and his colleagues were quick to dispel what they termed misconceptions. They explained, as present-day operators of the polygraph still do, that the testing of a suspect begins with a long series of innocuous questions in no way hinting at the offense. Not until a normal level of reaction has been recorded does the examiner abruptly pose the "dynamite question" relating directly to the crime.

Larson, who in later years recorded many of his experiments in his book *Lying and Its Detection*, relates the case of a housewife who reported the theft of a $20 bill from her home, which apparently had been entered by forcing open a window. The police, without a clue, questioned a number of people, including a family friend regarded as above suspicion, though he was known to have been the last person leaving the house. He finally agreed to a lie-detector test, declaring that he would be quickly exonerated. He promptly answered "no" when asked point blank if he had stolen the money, but the recording needle jumped far from the normal lines. Still the family would not believe him guilty.

The experiment was repeated on the following day with the same results. Advised of this, the family friend broke down and confessed the theft, remarking that "the machine has the goods on me."

Larson and other lie-detector experts relate similar experiences. Use of the technique has increased immeasurably in spite of criticism based mainly on the fact that subjects, bound with tapes and other necessary paraphernalia, become nervous and tense, leading sometimes to unfair and inaccurate results.

It was this persistent claim that moved the three inventors of the Psychological Stress Evaluator to look for a simpler way of detecting lies, one that not only would be easier to operate but, more importantly, would spare the subject from the physical entanglements that cause emotional strain and, consequently, incorrect recordings.

Their process completely eliminates the use of restraining tapes and cords. Instead, the subject merely speaks into a microphone or his voice is recorded by other means on magnetic tape which, in turn, is fed into a machine as small as a portable typewriter.

The product is manufactured at the Springfield plant, approximately twenty miles from Washington. A part of the building is used for training recruits in the operation of the Evaluator.

A branch office functions in Fort Lauderdale, Florida, while western headquarters are maintained in Los Angeles by the Barnes Investigation Agency, which offers courses to trainees as well as serving as a sales branch. The equipment costs approximately $3,200.

The principles behind PSE and its equipment are best detailed by quoting the Barnes Agency itself. "When one speaks," the organization explains, "the voice has two modulations—audible modulation and inaudible. The audible portion is what we hear. The inaudible modulation comes from the involuntary areas (those not directly controlled by the brain or thought processes). Internal stress is reflected in the inaudible variations of the voice. These differences *cannot* be heard, *but* they *can* be detected and recorded by the PSE.

"The key to successful use of the PSE is the preparation of simple selected questions keyed to the individual and structured to reveal normal or truthful answers and responses that are false. Once the personal pattern has been established any evasive or false answers reveal stress; if a person is not telling the truth, then analysis of his voice pattern will show it."

In still further explanation, the PSE sponsors state:

"Superimposed on the audible voice are inaudible frequency modulations. The FM quality of the voice is susceptible to the amount of stress that one may be under in speaking. To the human ear, a person may sound perfectly normal, free of tremors or 'guilt-revealing' sound variations. The PSE senses the differences and records the changes in the inaudible FM qualities of the voice on a chart. When the chart is interpreted by an experienced examiner, it reveals the key stress areas of the person being questioned."

The PSE backers are eager to explain the advantages of their product over other instruments used for detecting lies, such as the lie detector. They point first to its simplicity; it has few moving parts, making it relatively easy to learn to operate. Its recorder provides a permanent record of the interview, making it possible to feed the tape into the charting machine at any subsequent time. Tapes can even be made over a telephone line and interpreted later.

Nor is the use of PSE confined to criminal investigations. It can be applied by business firms for employee screening, employee morale, and efficiency of performance.

The inventors tell of the various tests undertaken in the initial development of their product. Of these they have this to say:

"The third test series was performed on actual subjects by a Maryland county police chief polygraph examiner using the

PSE-1 and the polygraph simultaneously. Truth-verification questioning techniques were employed, as well as a complex test structure, inasmuch as 'guilty knowledge' as well as innocence and guilt were of interest to the police department. Twenty-six cases containing 162 relevant elements have been corroborated by confession or investigation. This series was a real-world high-test situation in which PSE-1 evaluation provided the subsequently corroborated correct results in all elements for a success figure of 100 percent."

The language spoken apparently has no effect on results, for the proponents of PSE claim that successful findings have been obtained with Greek, Spanish, German, Italian, Arabic (Syrian and Iranian), Chinese Mandarin and Vietnamese subjects.

The Maryland tests already referred to have been followed by extensive and successful use of PSE by the police department in Howard County of that state, conducted under the direction of Lieutenant Michael P. Kradz, who has since resigned to assume an executive position with the Dektor company.

In citing a few illustrative cases in which he functioned as PSE examiner during his years in police service, Kradz takes satisfaction in the fact that innocent people wrongly accused were vindicated, while in others the guilty were convicted and punished.

There is, for example, the case of Jerome Goodman who was arrested on charges of attempted murder and burglary in Ellicott City, Maryland, in October, 1971. Though he had been named as an accomplice by one of three men jailed for breaking into a home and shooting a resisting resident, Goodman vigorously denied his guilt. In the absence of incriminating evidence, other than a prisoner's unsupported accusation, State's Attorney Richard Kinlein joined with Goodman's lawyer, Thomas C. Lloyd, in requesting a PSE test. So positive were the machine's indications that the accused man was truthfully pleading his innocence, that Circuit Court Judge T. Hunt May dismissed the charges and ordered the prisoner's immediate release. (He had been incarcerated for four months, awaiting trial.)

Four months later, in the same county, Robert L. Mills met a different fate. Jailed as a shoplifter, he insisted that he was a victim of mistaken identity and could easily prove his innocence before a jury.

Thirty minutes before his trial was scheduled to begin, Mills was persuaded by his attorney, Public Defender Bernard Goldberg, to undergo a PSE test. Kradz obtained the defendant's answers to a group of key questions and fed the tape into the graph-producing machine. Shortly afterward the officer was at the telephone calling the public defender. "The test is over," he reported. "It definitely indicates deception; you should see the upward lines made when he answered questions pertaining to the case."

Opening of the trial was delayed to permit a conference between Mills and his lawyer. An hour later the accused man stood before the court and pleaded guilty.

Early in May, 1972, Dolores King was puzzling the police with an explanation of why she had been arrested on charges of passing worthless checks in two Maryland counties, Baltimore and Howard. She told the authorities that she was innocent; that someone had forged her name to the spurious checks, a story that detectives were disinclined to believe.

After some discussion State's Attorney Kinlein and Public Defender Goldberg agreed to let a PSE test under Kradz' direction solve the question. The accused woman readily consented.

When the police examiner had finished scrutinizing the graphs made from the defendant's answers to direct questions involving the charges, he concluded that Dolores King had spoken the truth.

He so advised the public defender who, in turn, informed Judge Thomas Kissel and moved for a dismissal. The motion was readily granted.

There are many other cases in Howard County illustrating the effectiveness of PSE tests. In some instances, Kradz points out, PSE examinations have actually saved taxpayers' money by producing confessions and thus avoiding long and expensive trials. To prove his point he cites five significant cases involving larceny and arson in which the accused admitted their guilt when confronted by PSE evidence that they were not speaking the truth during their examinations.

The California murder in which PSE played a significant role, concerns the death of Mrs. Gloria Carpenter, a fifty-nine-year-old beautician, whose nude body was found submerged in a bathtub in her apartment in the city of Modesto at about two o'clock in the afternoon of May 1, 1973.

The grim discovery was made by Mrs. Carpenter's daughter, Bonnie Johnson, who went anxiously to her mother's apartment after repeated telephone calls had brought no response. She found the front door locked and was obliged to gain entrance with a pass key borrowed from the manager.

Her first thought was that her mother had died of a heart attack, a surmise shared by a police officer whom she had summoned. However, they became suspicious when it was found that two other locks on the same door were unfastened—Mrs. Carpenter was in the habit of securing all of the locks upon retiring for the night.

Despite this peculiar circumstance, fear of foul play was not confirmed until the arrival of Deputy Coroner William Fanter, who detected a thin line around the dead woman's neck. An autopsy later revealed that death had been due to strangulation, and it was surmised that a nylon stocking found on the bathroom floor had been used by the killer.

Further examination by the county pathologist, Dr. William Ernoehazy, disclosed that the victim had been raped. He fixed the time of death at about 12:30 that morning, and he was certain that she had succumbed before being immersed in the bathtub, because her lungs were free of water. The murderer, in the opinion of the police, had deliberately tried to make it appear that his victim had died of natural causes while bathing.

There were other curious elements surrounding the case. No signs of forcible entry to the apartment could be found nor was anything in disarray. Robbery obviously was not the motive, and the theory of a sex crime was strengthened when it was learned that Mrs. Carpenter had complained months before of an attempt to rape her by someone she had met in a bar.

Detectives, groping for a clue, set out to learn where Mrs. Carpenter had been the night before her death. They were told that she had been seen in a tavern late that night with a male companion known there as Jimmy Wayne Glenn.

This man, located a short time later, readily admitted that he had been drinking with her, but he insisted that he had left her at her door shortly before midnight and had not entered her apartment; in fact he asserted that he never had set foot in the place. He said further that after bidding Mrs. Carpenter good-night, he had gone directly to his own home in a far-removed unit of the sprawling 20th-Century Apartment complex and quickly retired.

A search of Glenn's rooms revealed a sinister circumstance. On a couch lay a detective magazine opened to a murder story in which the plot matched the killing of Mrs. Carpenter. While Glenn insisted that this was mere coincidence, police became increasingly suspicious, wondering whether a piece of fiction might have suggested the crime that they were trying to solve.

Reviewing what they knew, detectives pondered the facts confronting them. They already knew that their suspect was known "as somewhat of a chaser," yet they realized that at this point they lacked sufficient evidence to bring formal charges, though all clues pointed to their suspect's guilt. If they could disprove Glenn's insistence that he had not been in the woman's apartment, an arrest would be justified.

During a lengthy discussion of the case with Lieutenant Orville House, in charge of homicide, someone suggested a PSE test, the police having been interested in the new process and eager to establish its value.

Whether Glenn would consent to such a procedure was questionable. Certainly he could not be compelled to face the test if he refused. It was finally decided to try.

Glenn was informed that if he was telling the truth, the machine would support him; if it found him to be lying he faced arrest. To the satisfaction of the investigators Glenn welcomed the idea with enthusiasm.

At headquarters he was given a tape recorder and asked many questions about his night out with Mrs. Carpenter, especially whether he had left her at her doorstep, as he claimed, or entered her home. Again he insisted that he had told the truth in his first statements. But the PSE produced a different story.

Glenn's tape-recorded words had not been fed long into the PSE machine when the graph needle began to swerve upward from its normal course. Soon it was jumping far above the level lines, convincing the investigators that Glenn was not telling the truth. It was the answer that the police wanted, for while they doubted that PSE evidence could be used in court, it did tell them convincingly that they were working in the right direction; that all they needed was more direct or circumstantial evidence.

Now, proceeding with their original inquiries, detectives found a faint palmprint on the rim of the bathtub. FBI experts reported that it matched that of Glenn, and when he was told of this he quickly changed his story, admitting for the first time that he had been in the apartment not only on the crucial night but several times before. The print, he tried to explain, was made that night when he slipped on the wet bathroom floor and grabbed the tub rim to pull himself to his feet.

On May 4, three days after the finding of the body, Glenn was arrested and charged with first-degree murder. The trial, which started on July 30, ended in a verdict of guilty and he was sent to prison under the state's indeterminate sentence law.

The Modesto police were gratified that PSE had confirmed their early suspicions and their original course of investigation, though they made it clear that their work was well under way before the tests.

The Carpenter murder, however, was preceded by even earlier use of PSE in California. Sometime before 1970 it became a valuable tool of the state's forestry service, which uses the new equipment to determine the guilt or innocence of arson suspects in forest fires.

Its introduction in this field was due to the interest of Dean L. Bennett, who has served more than fifteen years as law-enforcement coordinator in the forestry department, with responsibility for protecting 200,000 acres of state parks from incendiary fires.

His statistics disclosed that 20 percent of all man-made fires in California are of incendiary origin; that each year thousands of cases of arson occur in fire-protected areas.

He knew also that arson is one of the most difficult crimes to prove because the evidence is usually destroyed by flames, while in many cases the culprit has ample time to escape before fire-fighting apparatus arrives. Suspects are picked up and questioned, though it is difficult to determine if they are telling the truth.

That is why Bennett decided to give the PSE method a trial. He is well satisfied with results. In 1972 alone, he says, fully fifteen puzzling cases were solved by the new technique, which made it possible either to eliminate a suspect or to proceed with his prosecution. Some have confessed after being confronted with evidence provided by the machine. "The most satisfactory results," he reports, "have come in interrogating kids."

So far he has not tried to introduce PSE graphs as evidence in court trials. "I am well pleased with PSE performance," he states, explaining that he regards it as a corroborating technique that reveals whether suspicions are well founded or groundless.

Bennett has his own tested theory as to the motivation for arson: in many instances it is a desire to clear an area for hunting; in others it is for what he calls "sexual gratification," motivation of this kind, he insists, is by no means rare.

There may be still further uses for PSE in the future if the vision—or imagination—of some enthusiasts comes to fruition. One writer, Roger M. Grace, in an article in a national magazine, suggests that independent observers, motivated only by personal interest, may have subjected the voices of Watergate witnesses to a check for truth, utilizing the new equipment. Grace wrote:

"Allan D. Bell Jr. (one of the inventors) said he would be 'very much surprised' if some owners of the PSE were not monitoring the televised hearings. . . .

"President Nixon's April 30, 1973, televised address on the Watergate affair was tape recorded by his agency, Bell said, but no analysis was made. The President's statements were not sufficiently definitive to secure a valid conclusion, he said."

Referring to a far different test of PSE, Grace concluded:

"The company's brochure boasts that 25 segments of television's *To Tell the Truth* were monitored, with a 94.7 percent record of accuracy in picking out the real John Doe from the pretenders. It is claimed that the accuracy level would have been higher if the show's segments were longer."

Like all other advances in scientific crime detection, PSE must stand the test of time. The final verdict on its effectiveness is still in the future.

Part 2

A
CORNUCOPIA
OF CRIME

X

An Ironic Surprise

A cruel fate made an ironic change in the surprise party planned to celebrate the thirty-second birthday of Neil LaFeve, a highly respected game technician and deputy warden in the Sensiba Wildlife Area in Sismico, Wisconsin, near the city of Green Bay. In consequence, what had been intended as a happy gathering of friends ended in tragedy, followed by a sensational trial that attracted wide attention throughout the state. The case also marked one of several motivated by passion that called for the help of Voiceprints.

It was Friday, September 24, 1971. LaFeve had left home in the early morning to patrol the preserve against game hunters, and his wife, Peggy, had turned at once to prepare for the night's event. Lest her carefully laid plans miscarry, she had asked her husband when he would return for dinner and he told her that it would be at the usual time, close to six o'clock. The guests, it was arranged, were to arrive shortly after six to offer their wishes for continued good health and long life. But LaFeve was never to see his wife and home again.

When the time for his expected return had come and passed, his wife became apprehensive, for LaFeve was known among his colleagues in the State Department of Natural Resources for his punctuality; in fact, he had never been late for dinner without first telephoning home to advise that some duty was detaining him.

Peggy LaFeve waited anxiously, fearful of trouble with poachers or an accident, but with the arrival of the first guests and still no sign of her husband, she decided to make such inquiries as she could. Turning to the telephone, she called his immediate superior, Harold Shine, who explained that early that day he had assigned LaFeve to post notices of a waterfowl closed section in the area. He assumed that this work would have been completed in only a few hours and he could not understand why his assistant was not already home.

Concealing his concern, he said that he would drive into the area at once for whatever information he could obtain. "Don't worry," he urged the young woman. "I'm sure we'll find that nothing serious has happened." The party guests, meanwhile, had left for home, offering whatever help they might give if it should become needed.

Shine started out hurriedly and drove along the roads where the signs were to be posted. They were all in place. At one point he detected foot tracks and followed them a short distance until they were lost in the dust. He explored a dike but nowhere could be found the slightest trace of his colleague.

For close to two more hours he continued his futile search over parts of the sixty acres of wilderness that makes up the game refuge, a region that few people care to visit. Then, realizing the uselessness of looking further in the darkness, he returned home and reported his failure to Mrs. LaFeve, now near the breaking point from worry. They agreed that she should call the sheriff's office immediately.

Sheriff Norbert Froelich lost no time in directing a relentless all-night search in which he and a corps of deputies were assisted by Wayne Truttman, chief investigator for Brown County and the officer in charge of the area. Aided by powerful searchlights, they moved from place to place but nowhere could they find any clue to the missing man. Fears for his safety were mounting fast.

At daybreak more officers were added to the posse as well as numbers of volunteers, men who knew LaFeve and were appalled by news of his disappearance.

By now the search had been thoroughly organized, with

plans that would take men in small groups over every foot of the ground. Orders were given to rope off many sections which would be kept closed to all but officers and volunteers.

One group of experienced helpers was assigned to start at Site 1, the farthest south, and to move slowly northward while other parties would fan out in different directions. Their orders were to beat the brush and to check thoroughly with metal detectors. Cars were stationed at strategic locations, and as bits of metal or other debris were picked up along the way they were rushed to the state crime laboratory for examination.

The search had continued for some time when one of the groups, working in a remote section a considerable distance from those at Site 1, came upon LaFeve's green pickup truck. A door was open as if its owner were to return at any moment. Inside the machine there was nothing to indicate what had happened to the missing driver. His tools and papers appeared to be intact but his absence immediately gave rise to still greater fears of foul play.

Meanwhile the searchers who had moved forward from Site 1 stopped suddenly at the excited shout of a man in the lead. "Get up here quick," he called to the others. "Here's something that looks pretty bad." He was pointing at a fairly large pool of blood.

The possemen scrambled forward, and as they did, the front man caught sight of a pair of spectacles half hidden in the dirt. Close by lay shattered sunglasses and a small sheet of paper. Then, as his companions gathered around him, he saw more blood and two exploded .22-caliber shell casings.

There was no further doubt of the missing warden's fate, and those who had found the grim evidence concluded that his body should not be far away.

They pressed on in the direction of Site 2, their eyes glued to the ground. Soon a gory sight confronted them. It was a small S-shaped path of blood extending over the ground and low shrubbery.

At the second site they found still more evidence of death. On a path lay a quantity of peculiar-looking white matter that looked as if it might be brain tissue. Then, as they moved carefully about, they discovered more blood spattered on trees and foliage. The mystery deepened when one of them took a tape from his pocket and observed that the red splotch on the tree trunks measured fully five feet from the ground.

"What a horrible life-and-death struggle must have happened here," a posseman remarked. Others nodded, too stunned for comment.

They were still contemplating their next move when a member of the party caught sight of a tooth and a small fragment of bone.

More convinced than ever that the body was in the immediate vicinity, the searchers tramped along in the direction of the next site but they could find no more blood spots or other evidence.

More than an hour of such careful scrutiny had passed when there came an excited cry from one of the men some yards away from his companions. "Look here, fellows," he exclaimed. "Loose earth in a parched section." To experienced outdoors men it was obvious that the ground had recently been opened.

They went to work with their hands, scooping earth away, fearful of using shovels or other implements. Soon they exposed a leg in a shallow grave, then a torso.

Before them lay a hideous sight. It was the decapitated body of Neil LaFeve!

They scanned the soil around them. Close by lay another grave. In it, near the surface, was the head of the ill-fated officer. It apparently had been severed with a spade or some other blunt tool. Piercing the skull were two bullet holes, and it appeared that shots had been fired into the torso, for there were gaping wounds and a few spent bullets on the ground.

Examining the narrow area around the graves, the searchers found tracks indicating that the body had been dragged for a surprisingly long distance, possibly by one or more persons looking for soft earth.

How and why had LaFeve met such a death? Who was responsible? These and other questions baffled those who had uncovered the reason for his disappearance. They would have to wait long for the answers.

Meanwhile runners were sent to headquarters to report the find and to arrange for the removal of the remains.

Discovery of the graves and the severed body, however, had solved only one phase of the mystery. Long weeks of exhaustive investigative work were to follow, and when the authorities finally found a suspect they were obliged to turn to three fields of science—Voiceprints, pathology, and ballistics—to determine his guilt or innocence.

Sheriff Froelich's first move, after the remains had been sent to the laboratory for pathological study, was to assign his most resourceful and tenacious investigator to direct the manhunt.

The man he selected was Sergeant Marvin Gerlikovski, and it was generally agreed that he was the best suited for the difficult task that lay ahead. With eighteen years of experience in law enforcement, he had proved his mettle in solving many baffling cases. He resided with his mother and had never married, and it was often said that he was wedded to the job of being a deputy sheriff. And those who envied his achievements were sometimes heard to comment that his persistence was quite understandable, for unlike most others he had no domestic responsibilities and could remain away from home as long as duty demanded, without thought of anyone but himself and the work before him.

In pursuing a clue, he followed it like a hound on the scent, and though self-educated in crime detection he displayed much of the knowledge and shrewdness attributed to those with college degrees in his field. He had the confidence of his associates, and his judgment was rarely, if ever, questioned. With this background, Gerlikovski accepted the challenge.

While those who had carried on the search for the missing warden had kept a sharp lookout for eyewitnesses or any kind of physical evidence, the sheriff's new appointee chose to take up the trail afresh, as if nothing had been done before. He directed that every foot of the refuge area be combed for clues and he covered much of the ground himself. But as days passed without result, he began contemplating the next step that he would follow, for the sergeant had his own ways of planning strategy.

"There's not a clue on the grounds," he reported to Sheriff Froelich one night. "The men have gone over every inch of it and they've found absolutely nothing."

"So what do you propose to do now?" Froelich inquired.

"The only thing that's left to do," retorted his trusted aide. "Somehow, I feel certain that poor LaFeve paid the penalty for an arrest in his line of duty. I'm going to check back—years back perhaps—on everyone he nabbed and every single person is going to have to prove his innocence."

"It's a big chore," the sheriff told him, "but go ahead. I'll give you all the help you need."

With a corps of willing workers, Gerlikovski started out on what proved to be a backbreaking task. Checking back over LaFave's record of arrests, he soon found written proof of what everyone had known—that the dead warden had been an unusually efficient officer, that in the past few years he had arrested scores of poachers and other violators. One of them, he reasoned, had probably sought revenge.

The task of locating and interrogating each and every person who had been arrested by LaFeve in the past few years soon proved more difficult than had been expected. Many had left the area; finding them consumed time and manpower. However, one by one they were made to appear before the sergeant or one of his men to be questioned as to their whereabouts during the time of the murder and disposal of the body.

In most instances, they were allowed to go after providing airtight alibis, but there were times when others, some far removed, had to be traced and checked to verify statements made to the officers.

From time to time an obdurate individual failed to satisfy his interrogator, who then asked permission for a lie-detector test. A polygraph and an experienced operator had been made available. The majority gladly accepted this opportunity to clear themselves; a few were reluctant, but in every case Froelich's ace detective succeeded in having his way. All of the results, however, were negative.

Gerlikovski seemed to be the least discouraged but he

realized that time was slipping by without material progress, excepting the steady elimination of those who might be suspect. He appeared to be buoyed by confidence that he was pursuing the proper course, though some of his helpers were remarking among themselves that he might be merely treading water. Similar doubts were being voiced by many volunteers who were moving about in quest of clues, spurred by a large reward offered for the apprehension of the killer.

Weeks of such frustrating work had passed when those who were still checking through the records came upon the name of a twenty-one-year-old man living in the area. He was Brian Hussong, and it was apparent that he had little or no respect for the law. Despite his age, he had been arrested several times by LaFeve for killing game in the refuge, his last offense having been only some months before when the warden caught him shooting pheasants. Obviously his first violation had not taught him a lesson.

Gerlikovski wondered whether at long last he might have come upon a worthwhile suspect. There was only one way to find out. Checking cautiously at first with those who knew the man, he was informed that Hussong was antisocial, showed little respect for law enforcement, and on occasion had voiced his strong dislike for LaFeve.

Locating him was not difficult. He was living at the home of his girl friend, Janice Obey, on the outskirts of the reservation.

Tall and muscular, with piercing brown eyes, dark hair unkempt, Hussong met the deputy with a sullen and defiant look, obviously resentful of the approach. Asked to explain where he had been during the hours that the murder was presumed to have occurred, he was evasive and sometimes contradictory. Parrying specific questions, he suggested that he "might have been" here or there. His only definite statements were that he knew nothing of the crime and that he never had possessed a gun.

His interrogator told him frankly that he was dissatisfied with the interview, explaining the eagerness of others to establish their alibis. "Some of them," Gerlikovski asserted, "even agreed to take lie-detector tests to prove their innocence. Why don't you do the same; if you're telling the truth the machine will prove it."

Hussong fairly bristled with anger at the suggestion. "I'll do nothing of the kind," he snapped. "I told you I didn't do it; that's enough. You damned well should take my word for it."

But the deputy was far from satisfied. There was nothing to do then but to dismiss the young man, but the investigator at last felt confident that he had struck pay dirt. How to prove his suspicions, however, was another matter, and he knew that the situation called for resourceful, intelligent thinking.

Despite his lack of academic training, he had read extensively in the field of scientific crime detection and was thoroughly familiar with all of the latest advances. The use of Voiceprints fascinated him, yet he did not anticipate that his routine work would afford an opportunity to resort to the new spectogram method. However, the more Gerlikovski pondered his problem, the more he wondered how Voiceprints could be utilized. Obviously voices had played no part in the case—but somehow, he reasoned, there might be a way to use them to support his grave suspicions.

He soon shared his thought with Sheriff Froelich and the newly elected prosecutor, Donald R. Zuidmulder. They listened attentively to the daring move that he was proposing.

"It's a bold idea all right," one of them remarked, "but can we get court permission? It's never been done before in Wisconsin."

"But it won't hurt to try," the deputy sheriff pressed. "What's wrong with putting it up to the judge and the attorney general? Nothing ventured, nothing gained."

The next day the three sat down with Circuit Judge Donald W. Gleason and Attorney General Robert W. Warren at a hastily called conference. The latter two were told of every step in the investigation and of the impasse that had been reached. They were informed that the only recourse lay in tapping Janice Obey's telephone, for it appeared probable that young Hussong, if guilty, was in communication with his relatives and friends for advice and help.

"It might produce worthwhile evidence," Gerlikovski argued, "and it might even give us an opportunity to use Voiceprints. Who knows?"

There was long discussion and in the end Judge Gleason told them that he would authorize the use of wire tapping, though such a step would set a legal precedent for the state.

Tapping of the girl's telephone presented little difficulty to Sergeant Larry Laes, who was familiar with such operations. Deputies in the sheriff's office were posted to listen in on a round-the-clock basis. Before long Hussong was overheard discussing his problems with his mother, Mary, and his eighty-three-year-old grandmother, Mrs. Agnes Hussong, who informed him that she had his guns securely hidden where no one could find them.

The deputies also listened to one conversation in which Hussong, talking from the outside to his girl friend, Janice, asked for her advice as to how he could recover the weapons. She had a plan which young Brian quickly rejected because "those damned pigs" were watching him.

And at times there were talks between mother and son about the best way for him to establish an alibi.

It was the grandmother's confidence about the hidden guns, however, that prompted an overt move by the authorities. Losing little time, they obtained a search warrant and Sergeant Gerlikovski led the party of officers to her home.

Her face paled when they identified themselves and inquired about the weapons. Realizing her situation, the aged woman decided to tell the truth and unburdened herself of her secret, revealing to the deputies the exact location of the cache.

Another search warrant was obtained and before the day was over the firearms were in the possession of the sheriff. They were turned over to William Rathman, the ballistics expert in the state crime laboratory at Madison, who already had testified in 165 other cases. Following customary procedures he fired test bullets from each of the weapons, studied the rifling marks, and finally concluded without doubt that the spent shells found at the scene of the murder had come from one of Hussong's guns. The time for an arrest had come.

A warrant was issued on a charge of first-degree murder, and Hussong was taken into custody at his parents' home, still protesting his innocence and claiming an alibi. It was December 16, 1971, nearly three months after the murder.

Sergeant Gerlikovski knew that he was ready to move on his original idea, though vague at the time, and resort to Voiceprints as a scientific means of clinching the case. Such a procedure had never before been followed in Wisconsin and there was doubt as to whether court permission could be obtained, but the prosecutor, Zuidmulder, was ready to try.

After detailed explanations, he succeeded in obtaining an order directing that each person who had been overheard talking with Brian, as well as the young defendant himself, be required to record his or her voice. Again the state had made a notable advance in crime detection.

Some of those involved were inclined to refuse, but they were informed that disobedience would mean contempt of court. So the tapes were obtained and with recordings of the original wire-tapped conversations they were rushed to Lieutenant Nash, heading the Voice Identification Unit of the Michigan State Police. Nowhere else in the country, or even in the world, did a police crime laboratory offer such facilities to those requiring them.

Nash went to work, converting the tapes into spectograms by the process he had used so many times before. Days later he reported to the anxious officials in Wisconsin that all of the recordings matched; he was fully convinced that the incriminating conversations had been carried on by those presumed to have been the speakers. It was the conclusion for which the prosecutor had been hoping, for he had looked to Voiceprints as most vitally important evidence.

The defense, having heard of the expert's findings, seemed unperturbed. Perhaps the jury would not be impressed by a new method of identification never used before in the state. Nevertheless, Voiceprints were to become one of the pivotal issues of the trial which began January 18 of the following year.

That morning Hussong, still in jail because he could not raise $75,000 bail, was led manacled before Judge John Jaekels for preliminary hearing. The proceedings, entirely perfunctory, ended briefly with an order holding the defendant for jury trial. This began in March before Circuit Judge Robert Parins, with the accused defended by Attorney James Oressentin, who had been appointed by the court.

In the opening hours Hussong lost the first of many legal skirmishes. His lawyer had fought hard for a change of venue, contending that public opinion would make a fair trial impossible. The plea was promptly denied. A jury of seven men and five women was impaneled and opening statements followed.

Donald Zuidmulder, the prosecutor, having carefully prepared his case in advance, began by calling a succession of witnesses to relate the events of the day of the murder and of the next, when the body was found. Mrs. LaFeve testified first about her husband's disappearance. She was followed by Sheriff Froelich and Sergeant Gerlikovski, who detailed the progress of the search and its grim ending. A pathologist told of the condition of the body, and Rathman, the ballistics expert, swore that his examination of bullets and casings, made with a high-powered stereoscopic microscope, proved that they had been fired from the defendant's guns. Another witness testified that he had seen one of Hussong's weapons in the back seat of his car on the day of the crime.

To the surprise of many in the crowded courtroom, the defendant's aged grandmother, pale and haggard, was called to the stand and questioned regarding the weapons she had admitted hiding. This time, however, she vehemently denied ever having told anyone that these had been in her possession or that she had cached them. While her appearance at this time was not then understood, it soon became apparent when the prosecutor called out:

"The state calls Lieutenant Nash to the witness chair."

Briskly stepping forward, the Michigan officer first explained his qualifications, then proceeded to tell in detail how he had convinced himself by spectogram comparisons that it was the grandmother who, in a taped telephone conversation, had admitted hiding the firearms.

Nash had still more to say. Responding to sharply pointed

questions by the prosecutor, he explained how Voiceprints had established the authenticity of the other voices heard over Hussong's taped telephone.

The defense, realizing that a climactic point in the trial had been reached, subjected the witness to gruelling cross-examination, but Nash stood his ground firmly and could not be made to deviate from his original testimony.

When court adjourned for the day newsmen crowded around Zuidmulder, inquiring what he intended to do about the grandmother's contradicted testimony. "Nothing," he replied, explaining that the aged woman was beloved by all who knew her and had acted only as most others would have under the circumstances. No one questioned his judgment.

Hussong took the stand in his own defense, denied his guilt, and did his best to account for his hour-by-hour movements on the day of the murder. Much of his testimony was corroborated by his mother, who said that he had spent the greater part of the day helping her can tomatoes.

The hands of the courtroom clock stood at exactly 9:27 on the morning of Thursday, April 13, 1972, when the jury retired after hearing seven days of testimony and closing arguments. The judge's instructions had emphasized the defendant's right to a presumption of innocence. With them, the jurors took a small model of the reservation area, with vital points involved in the case carefully marked.

A quick verdict was expected and many remained in the courtroom. They were misled, however, by a knock on the jury-room door at ten o'clock. Instead of announcing a verdict, the jurors asked that they be permitted to hear all of the tape recordings, a request that convinced officials and spectators that Voiceprint testimony had become a major issue in the initial period of deliberations.

Two and a half hours had passed since the jury's retirement when a second knock announced that a verdict had been reached. Hussong, who had followed all of the proceedings with a bored expression, appeared to be disinterested as the men and women filed back into the box.

Moments later Judge Parins scanned the slip of paper

handed to him and began to read. Hussong had been found guilty of first-degree murder. There was no recommendation for clemency despite his youth.

Members of the convicted man's family burst into tears, though the defendant showed no signs of emotion.

Judge Parins thanked the jurors for their services and informed them that they were under no obligation to discuss the verdict with anyone. It was an unnecessary statement, for the twelve men and women explained later that they had reached such an agreement before returning their verdict.

For the state, District Attorney Zuidmulder said he was gratified by the results of the trial but took no personal satisfaction in sending so young a man to prison for the remainder of his life. He thanked all who had assisted in the gathering of evidence, especially Nash and the Michigan State Police for providing the Voiceprint evidence.

Attorney Oressentin, who had defended Hussong, inquired as to necessary procedures in filing an appeal.

After the jurors had left the courtroom, Judge Parins asked the convicted man to stand. "Have you anything to say before sentence is pronounced?" he inquired.

Hussong, stern-faced, replied: "What's to say?" Then he slipped back into his chair. No one commented on the three-word answer.

Judge Parins told the young man to stand again. This time he was sentenced to serve the balance of his life in the state's prison system. The Wisconsin State Reformatory was designated as the reception center.

Court attendants later estimated that the earliest parole possible would not come until Hussong had served a minimum of slightly less than twelve years.

Defense counsel lost no time in filing its first appeal, contending that the trial judge had erred in denying a motion for a change of venue based on community prejudice. It was claimed further that the evidence did not warrant a conviction.

The appeal was promptly denied, and as Hussong listened to the decision he commented: "This is a bigger joke than the trial was."

At this writing the case has been carried to the State Supreme Court, which still has the matter under consideration.

Ironically, the state has formally presented Hussong with a bill for $16,181 owing to the court-appointed defense lawyer for his services. It means that if the convicted murderer, unemployed at the time of his arrest, should ever be freed and employed gainfully, he would begin his new life with a huge debt over his head.

XI

The High Cost of Sex

If one were to search for the most bizarre and comical case ever solved by Voiceprints, the hunt would end not in the United States but in Switzerland, where the technique has been in practical use for several years as a result of Kersta's personal contacts with that country's top criminal justice authorities. In fact, it was Kersta who introduced his work there and continues an ongoing relationship when advice becomes necessary.

Switzerland, however, is not the only foreign nation to which he has introduced Voiceprints. Australia and England are among the others.

The strange and amusing case, with sex as its dominating element, is related by Dr. E. P. Martin, head of the Technical Criminal Division of the District Attorney's Office in Basle, in a published article written in German and intended to illustrate the diversity of cases which his department has solved through the use of the Kersta method.

Martin is careful to point out that the case he cites is of special interest because it was the first based essentially on a recorded voice to be presented to a Swiss court. He does not identify the principals, obviously for reasons of his own, but the facts, rather than the names involved, justify a retelling of the story with some pardonable degree of dramatization.

It began in the Basle offices of a well-known Swiss business firm where an employee in a relatively minor position approached his boss with a request for a small financial loan. "What do you need it for?" he was asked. "We are paying you a good salary and you're not married."

The other explained that he had arranged for a few days vacation and had planned to spend it in a neighboring town.

To the young employee's surprise he was immediately handed 500 Swiss francs without further questioning, but there was a noticeable twinkle in the lender's eye.

"I'm lending this to you on one condition," the head of the firm explained with no show of embarrassment. "In return for this loan I'd like the use of your apartment while you're away."

The other, with a curious look on his face, nodded his approval. "Of course you can use my apartment while I'm gone," he said, "but I don't understand. You have a nice home—and a wife and children."

Before answering, the other winked and laughed. "Sure I've got a home and a family, but a few days of fun in your place with some girl friends will break the monotony of things. Okay?"

The deal was closed as an apparently friendly, if unusual, bargain, but the older man had no way of even guessing the sinister plans running through the bachelor's mind at the time. He did not know that he was dealing with a man who, completely devoid of moral scruples, was fully determined to find out what would be going on in the apartment during his absence and who would be his boss's companions.

His scheme was bold and daring; ungentlemanly to say the least.

Quickly, with devilish amusement, he bought a tape recorder that would run for a considerable time. This he concealed under his bed, resorting to his own ingenuity to adjust an electrical timer to the instrument. This way he would have some record of what occurred in the borrowed suite.

Thinking he was safe, the unfaithful businessman made merry while his employee was away and gladly handed back the keys when the owner returned. "I'm quite indebted to you," he said gratefully. "I really had a very good time."

What he did not know, however, was the story that the tape recorder revealed—the employer had occupied the apartment not with women of his own age or close to it but with the very young girl apprentice in the business—and she was a minor.

The secret remained well guarded by the young man, but all respect for his boss had vanished. Their relationship deteriorated fast; there were clashes with increasing frequency until at last, about a year later, the young employee was summarily fired.

It was then that the man without a job suddenly realized his opportunity for revenge. He had a secret weapon and he wondered if he should use it. He consulted his friends and found them of mixed minds. Some told him that what he planned would be a dastardly thing to do; others encouraged him.

In the end he chose to follow his own inclinations. He went to the police and swore to a complaint charging his former boss with seducing a minor and he proudly explained the nature of the evidence he could produce to prove his accusation.

His announcement created a sensation. The accused, popularly known as a sedate businessman and a highly respected head of a family, became the object of public ridicule. The case quickly received newspaper attention and in some quarters the defendant was mocked and jeered.

Friends and curious spectators gathered in the courtroom when the accused man appeared. His lawyers freely admitted the authenticity of the damning tape recordings—but to a degree. They insisted that the feminine voice was not that of the minor girl but of a woman of mature age, an old friend. If this were so the case obviously would collapse and, of course, there was a simple and scientific way of ascertaining the truth—Voiceprints.

The judge accordingly ordered that a recording of the minor apprentice's voice be made for comparison with the tapes taken from the bedroom. When this was accomplished a few days later, the authorities, new to the use of Voiceprints, decided to send the tapes directly to Kersta's laboratory in New Jersey, confident that they could depend on his expertise in reaching a definite opinion.

A week later the American scientist reported that he compared spectograms of the two voices and was positive that they were of the same person—the girl who was a minor.

The defense, however, was reluctant to give up without further struggle. Promptly lawyers for the accused came forward with a charge that the tapes deliberately had been falsified, but their contention fell on deaf ears, for the court contended that a defense based on possible fraud was not admissible. So, in consequence, the philanderer paid well for his folly.

Two other cases ending in convictions, both less sensational and along the pattern of those tried in America with Voiceprint evidence, also are cited by Dr. Martin in his lengthy and interesting paper. In it, he joins enthusiastically in his support of the effectiveness of Voiceprint testimony.

Referring to the Switzerland trials, Martin points out that the court in each instance drew a clear distinction between tape recordings and Voiceprint evidence, contending that the former can be falsified by a skilled technician while Voiceprints cannot. This conclusion, he states, was reached by the judges after lengthy correspondence with Kersta, who assured them that any attempt at tampering by cutting, reassembling or making insertions into tapes would be detected at once by the spectograms. They have been shown to be foolproof, he contended.

Martin, in still another paper, cites an experiment made with the help of Elliot Reid, a professional entertainer, who imitated the voice of President Nixon so perfectly that a tape recording fooled a panel of experienced listeners. The voice spectogram, however, left no doubt as to which was the genuine voice.

"It is confidently expected," Martin wrote in conclusion, "that voice identification by electronic means will eventually be accepted."

XII

Graphs Bring a Confession

Young Lawrence Vice had just made a serious decision, though he still had time to change his mind.

Seated in a courtroom in Charleston, South Carolina, he would be called on momentarily to enter his plea to a charge of voluntary manslaughter in what was a crime of passion. It would be his second trial, for his conviction months before had been reversed by appellate judges on technical grounds.

Vice knew that Lieutenant Ernest W. Nash, the Voiceprint expert from Michigan, had been summoned to Charleston to appear as a key witness for the prosecution, and this meant, of course, that Voiceprint evidence would be used strongly against the defense.

For the harried defendant it was time for quick thinking. Should he plead guilty to killing a man, spare himself from the damning testimony of the expert, and throw himself on the mercy of the court? Or should he gamble on the possibility that a jury might disagree over highly technical scientific testimony? It was for Vice to make his own choice.

The case had a grim beginning on Sunday morning, March 16, 1969. At exactly 7:15 a newspaper delivery boy, walking into the yard of a rooming house at 76 George Street in Charleston, had recoiled at the sight of the blood-stained body of a youngish-looking man lying fully clothed on the ground. He ran to the nearest telephone and in ten minutes the police were on the scene.

They first made certain that the victim was dead; then called for the coroner. A hasty examination of the body disclosed several stab wounds that accounted for the fact that both the chest and left leg were saturated with blood. No weapon was in sight.

As the officers began their questioning of tenants in the building, they learned that the corpse was that of Robert Farrow, who had lived alone on the first floor of the two-story structure. Further inquiries disclosed details of a bitter quarrel between the deceased and another lodger during the night, though the identity of the latter appeared to be unknown.

Surprising news came, however, when a policeman reached the last room on the second floor and found the door locked from the outside with a hasp and padlock. The approach was covered with blood and a gory trail led down a stairway from this room to that of the murdered man. The occupant of the locked room was identified as Lawrence Vice, but apparently he had disappeared. No one knew the time of his departure or when he would return.

Several in the building related that at a late hour on the previous night Farrow had returned in an intoxicated condition and was overheard arguing heatedly with another roomer. Angry talk had been followed by sounds of a fierce struggle between the two until one man cried out that he was going upstairs and would return shortly. Heavy footsteps were heard on the stairs and soon afterward the struggle was resumed, only to end moments later in complete silence.

While exact details of this occurrence were being carefully rechecked, one of the officers called headquarters to request help from the Homicide Bureau. In return he was told of an earlier incident of which he had no knowledge.

Shortly after one o'clock that morning, he was informed, headquarters had received an anonymous telephone call. A man addressing the desk sergeant, but refusing to give his name, had said: "I'm down at 76 George Street, downstairs, and a man has been seriously crushed in the damned stomach." The message, as a matter of procedure, had been recorded on tape.

An officer in a radio car had rushed to the scene but he could find no trace of a body. On his return he had listened to the recording and had suspected that it might be the voice of Lawrence Vice, with whom he was acquainted. The call had been noted on the blotter for further investigation in the morning.

Continued investigation at the scene of the crime that morning revealed still more evidence confirming the coroner's opinion that death had occurred between midnight and six o'clock, presumably about the time that the scuffle had been heard. Four knife wounds had been inflicted, one of them penetrating the heart.

Newly found clues included a "praying hands" medallion that Vice was known to wear constantly on a chain. Now it had been picked up in a pool of blood close to Farrow's door. Near this lay the victim's hat and the cane always carried by Farrow, who was crippled and could walk only with support.

A citywide search for Vice was already under way and as it continued, detectives, eager for still further evidence, ordered the landlady to open the door of Vice's room with a passkey. Bloodspots found inside were photographed—a legal error it later developed, for the officers in their haste had failed to obtain a search warrant, though they believed their action to be justified. This move alone was ultimately to win a new trial for the defendant.

The intensive hunt for Vice ended two days later when he walked into police headquarters, surrendered, and was booked on a charge of murder. He denied his guilt but refused to answer specific questions despite the fact that keys in his possession were spotted with blood, his face was bruised, and he was not wearing the medallion. A four-inch knife, which was usually in his pocket, was missing, leading investigators to believe that this was the lethal weapon, though it still could not be found.

To bolster the charge lodged against Vice and to obviate unnecessary court delays, the authorities took the case to the grand jury and an indictment was promptly returned.

At this point, however, the police and county solicitor reviewed their case and realized that it was based solely on what was regarded as strong circumstantial evidence. There were no eyewitnesses to the killing, and if further support were needed it could come only from the crime laboratory, where technicians had already been busily at work. Fingernail scrapings from the victim's right hand had revealed the presence of human blood, but it was insufficient to be typed. Blood samples from Farrow's body had been compared with specimens from the flooring. Both were Type O, a significant point, yet lacking the relevance to impress a jury.

The prosecution turned now to voice comparisons, but with no intention of using Voiceprints, though its reasoning on this point was not explained. No doubt the lawyers feared that the new method would not receive court acceptance. However, formal notice was served by the state on Vice, informing him that he would be required to speak through the police telephone and a taping machine so that his voice could be compared with the anonymous call on the night of the murder. Vice flatly refused, but the prosecution was determined to press its demands at a later time.

The trial finally began in General Sessions Court, with the defendant boasting that he would be free in a few days. Proceeding slowly step by step, the prosecution wove a tight net of circumstantial evidence against the defendant, as one tenant of the rooming house after another repeated accounts of the late-night struggle already told to the police.

They were followed by detectives and laboratory technicians explaining the significance of the blood stains in their incriminating locations. As if this were not enough, the state sprung a surprise, disclosing that Vice had tried to induce his landlady to testify that she had sent him downstairs on the night of the trouble "to quiet some quarrel," but she had flatly refused to do his bidding.

Now the state turned again to the issue of voice comparisons. Its formal demand that the defendant be ordered to record his voice was granted by the court and during a recess, when the jury had been excused, Vice, over the objection of his counsel, was required to speak into a police telephone for recording over the same machine that had taped the message from the unidentified caller.

The defense fumed when the court announced that both recordings would be admitted in evidence, and in the presence of the jury the two tapes were played so that the men and women in the box could make their own comparisons. Nor did the state stop there. With the judge's permission and over further defense objections, a police officer who had known Vice was allowed to testify that he considered both voices to be of the man on trial. This testimony also was vigorously attacked by Vice's counsel on the grounds that this lawman was not qualified to pass accurate judgment.

Vice chose not to testify in his own behalf, and his lawyers contented themselves with an attack on the nature of the circumstantial evidence and on the manner in which much of it had been obtained.

The jury deliberated only a relatively short time. When its verdict was read Vice was found guilty of voluntary manslaughter instead of murder. A few days later he was sentenced to serve twenty years in prison. But the legal fight was far from ended.

The defense immediately served notice of appeal to be based on three major claims of error by the trial judge. It was contended that the police had violated the defendant's rights by entering his lodgings without a search warrant and that therefore evidence of blood stains found and photographed there should have been barred at the trial. The second attack was on the tape recordings, and lastly it was argued that the trial court erred in denying a defense motion for a directed verdict of not guilty.

The decision of the supreme court, when it finally came, was a decided victory for the defense, though many lawyers found significance in the judges' approval of the General Sessions Court in permitting the voice comparisons, as conducted by ear, as legal evidence. As already stated, Voiceprints had not been introduced at the trial.

The supreme court, upholding the first contention of the defense, ruled that entry into a defendant's room without a search warrant was unlawful. It held "that where officers engaged in investigation of homicide about five hours after discovery of a dead body traced bloodspots to the door of defendant's room which was locked with a padlock from the outside and there was no circumstance upon which to base conclusion that exigencies of the situation required dispensing with necessity of a warrant to search defendant's room, search of room after being admitted by landlady was illegal and admission of evidence of blood in defendant's room was not harmless error." Many earlier decisions were cited in support of this position, which some legal authorities regarded as a highly significant desire by the judges to grant a defendant every possible protection under the law.

Based on this judgment, the high court, in passing on the trial court's denial of a directed not guilty verdict, ruled that "appellant maintains that the evidence was insufficient to establish his guilt and that his motion for a directed verdict of not guilty should have been granted by the trial judge. In considering this question, the evidence obtained as a result of the unlawful search of appellant's room must, of course, be disregarded."

On the issue of the voice comparisons the supreme court justices took an opposite view to defense contentions. They stated:

"The requirement that appellant speak into the telephone so that his voice could be recorded for identification purposes did not violate his privileges against self-incrimination. . . .

"Neither did the admission of the voice recording deprive appellant of due process. The recording was made of appellant's voice while speaking into the telephone and on the same machine that recorded the voice of the anonymous caller. The statement which appellant was required to make and the circumstances surrounding the two recordings were such as to afford the jury a reasonable basis for comparison of the voices recorded. There is nothing to indicate that the admission of the recording deprived appellant of due process or in any way violated his constitutional right to a fair trial."

Nevertheless, on the other disputed points raised by Vice's

counsel, the court reversed the judgment of the trial jury and ordered a new trial. Vice and his attorneys hailed their success and the accused man again told newsmen that he was certain of acquittal.

In preparation for the second court struggle, Robert E. Wallace, solicitor for the Ninth Judicial Circuit in Charleston, decided that this time he would invoke the use of Voiceprints. Already having recordings of the anonymous telephone caller and of Vice's own voice, he sent them to Lieutenant Nash in East Lansing, Michigan, and requested that they be compared by the spectogram process.

As Wallace related to this writer: "He [Nash] advised me that the voices were the same."

The appeals court already having ruled on the admissibility of voice recordings, the solicitor felt certain that he would encounter no legal difficulty in producing Nash as his main witness.

Arrangements were made to bring him to Charleston, and when the prosecution's time had come following selection of a jury and opening preliminaries, Lieutenant Nash was in Charleston waiting to be called to the courtroom. But the summons never came.

At the appropriate moment, Vice was ordered to stand before the presiding judge.

"Lawrence Vice," intoned the court, "you are charged with voluntary manslaughter. Are you guilty or not guilty?"

Almost a full minute passed before his voice was heard. Through his mind, no doubt, flashed thoughts of what the Voiceprint expert would say, for Vice was known to have learned the results of Nash's tests. The accused man had already professed his innocence but now only a moment remained to change his mind, if he so chose.

At last his lips began to move and in little more than a whisper he was heard to utter the one word "Guilty."

Though it had been unnecessary to introduce Voiceprints into the testimony, they had the telling impact Solicitor Wallace had hoped for.

Lieutenant Nash took the next plane back to Michigan. It was time for Vice to receive his sentence.

He was more fortunate than he had expected. The court committed him to serve three years in state's prison. He remained there for little more than sixty days when he applied for parole, claiming that he was eligible because of the total time he had been in custody since his arrest.

His petition was granted and Vice walked out of his cell a free man, subject only to the legal parole restrictions.

XIII

Ma Bell Provides a Clue

In Minnesota, lawyers still discuss the unique case of an attractive young St. Paul woman who saved herself from a murderer's cell by telling the truth after Voiceprints had trapped her in deliberate lies. Had it not been for spectograms of her voice and a sympathetic jury, she well might have spent the remainder of her life branded as a "cop killer."

Though it is another case involving a mysterious phone call, the proceedings are extraordinary in a number of other ways. They support Lawrence Kersta's contention that Voiceprints are just as effective in ferreting out the truth as the polygraph, fingerprints, and truth serum.

Of course, Constance Louise Trimble might not have been so fortunate had she not learned before her trial that a picture of her voice had revealed her falsehoods. Only then did a guilty conscience and practical reasoning convince her that "honesty is the best policy."

The case of the *People* vs. *Trimble* also made legal history, for, as the Criminal Law Reporter of the Bureau of National Affairs stated a short time later: "The Minnesota Court is the first civilian appellate court to approve the use of spectograph evidence."

1224CORNUCOPIA OF CRIME

It was a strange combination of circumstances that led to Miss Trimble's arrest and trial on a murder charge. Shortly after midnight on May 22, 1970, the quiet of the St. Paul police headquarters was suddenly broken by the sharp ringing of the telephone. A desk sergeant answered and listened to the voice of an apparently agitated woman appealing for help. "Please send an officer at once to 859 Hague Avenue," the caller requested. "There's a woman there in an awful state. Please send . . ."

"What seems to be the trouble?" the policeman inquired.

"This woman's pregnant . . . about to deliver . . . and she's all alone."

That ended the conversation and within minutes Patrolmen Glen Kothe and James Sackett were speeding on their way in a radio car.

Arriving at the scene, they scrambled up the front stairs of a poor-looking frame dwelling and knocked on the door. There was no response.

Presuming that the troubled woman was unable to answer, Kothe hurried on a narrow graveled pavement to the back door while his partner remained in front. Kothe had barely reached the rear of the house when he heard a shot and saw a blinding flash in the darkness. Rushing around to the front, he saw Officer Sackett lying on the ground, blood flowing from a large wound in his head.

"What's happened?" Kothe asked. Sackett's lips moved but no sound came.

Kothe's first move was to run to his car and call for an ambulance. His partner died on the way to the hospital without regaining consciousness. An examination showed that he had been shot with a high-caliber revolver.

His death created a furor in St. Paul police circles. Sackett had been a favorite in the department, a dedicated officer who knew no fear and several times had risked his life in the line of duty.

Though quick death had sealed his lips, detectives reasoned that he had been shot from ambush moments after his partner had left his side. Though there was no apparent reason for the killing, they quickly scanned his most recent arrest reports hoping in vain that some case might reveal a motive. That, however, was only one of many moves begun at once to find the murderer.

Squads of men, working with powerful searchlights, combed the neighborhood for clues. Road blocks were set up and orders were broadcast to officers throughout the city to look for suspicious characters. Careful search of the entire area failed to reveal the murder weapon.

During the night and far into the next morning the futile search continued. Here and there a loiterer was stopped, sharply questioned, and finally allowed to go when he satisfied an officer that he knew nothing of the crime.

Modern science, however, had provided the first valuable clue. Because the St. Paul police, like their counterparts in almost every other large city, use tape machines to preserve all emergency calls regardless of their nature, the authorities had a permanent record of the mysterious woman's voice, but they fully realized the problem confronting them in putting it to practical use.

Actually their task was to find the one woman from among St. Paul's population of well over 313,000 people whose voice they had on magnetic tape. It would be a needle-in-a-haystack hunt, but they were determined that the wanton killing of a beloved brother officer must be avenged.

As the investigation continued, with no clue but a few recorded words, detectives began to focus attention on a small gang of militant young men who frequented the Hague Avenue neighborhood. None of them had ever been in trouble with the law, but neighbors had occasionally complained of difficulties with a few who recklessly rode their motorcycles over lawns or carved their initials in garden trees. Because members of such gangs usually consort with young women, the police turned to a meticulous checking of those of both sexes.

Just how the detectives came upon a suspect is a guarded secret among them; perhaps someone with a grudge had whispered into an eager ear. At all events, the name of Connie Trimble suddenly became an important element in the case.

Miss Trimble, an unusually attractive young woman of

twenty, slim and vivacious, had no police record. She was known to be the mother of a two-year-old daughter born out of wedlock.

Acting on only scant information, the investigators sent for her, hoping that she might provide some lead of value. She faced the officers willingly, agreeing that she would gladly answer all of their questions truthfully, for, as she explained, she would ask nothing more than a chance to help in solving so heinous a crime.

As to the telephone call that led to the murder she vehemently denied that she had made it, or, in fact, knew anything about it. "Why should I have done such a thing?" she insisted. "I really don't know anything about it, and that's gospel truth."

Despite so firm a denial, they grilled her for hours, hoping to catch her in a contradiction, but without success. Through it all she parried every question until at last the police told her to go home; she might hear from them later.

The investigators, however, were far from satisfied. Several thought that they detected a similarity between her voice and that on the tape, the police station recording that they had listened to so many times. To be absolutely certain, and in fairness to Miss Trimble, they agreed that it would be necessary to obtain a record of her voice and that this could be done only by resorting to a ruse. In other words, they would have to tape her voice without her knowing it.

Various schemes were proposed and abandoned as impractical. In the end it was decided to question her about her status as a welfare recipient, a ruse that they considered justified.

Such a move, however, required legal sanction. Its purpose was explained to District Judge Stephen Maxwell by Officer Earl Miels of the St. Paul Police Homicide Division, who had been taking an active part in the case.

Judge Maxwell listened attentively and soon gave his approval. The next step was up to the police.

For its execution a resourceful policewoman, Carolen Bailey, was selected and carefully briefed on her assignment. Following instructions, she telephoned Connie Trimble, requesting a meeting in the offices of the Ramsey County Welfare

Department to discuss certain important "eligibility factors" involved in the young woman's monthly checks.

With no reason to suspect the true reason for the summons, Miss Trimble appeared at the welfare offices on the following day and was met by Policewoman Bailey in plainclothes, prepared to play her role as a welfare official. A tape recorder had been secreted under a desk in a way that it could be turned on as soon as the conversation started.

Miss Trimble answered all of the inquiries put to her and was finally told that she could leave. The ruse had produced the desired results.

Without delay, the tape recording was sent airmail to Detective Lieutenant Nash for comparison with the recorded voice of the woman caller, who it was believed was responsible for Officer Sackett's death.

Nash followed the usual procedure of converting the taped voices into spectograms and hours were spent in an intensive line-for-line study of the graphs.

While Nash himself felt reasonably certain of the similarity between the two voices, he was not yet ready to officially make known his judgment, realizing that a woman's liberty was at stake. With thoroughness and caution, he telephoned to the St. Paul police requesting them to secure for him tape recordings of other women and girls who had been Connie Trimble's companions.

This naturally required further resourcefulness, but in the end, through ways of their own, the police obtained tapes of thirteen other voices and rushed them to Nash.

Again he turned to the usual technical procedures, experimenting not with one but with more than a dozen other recordings, each to be compared with that of the original caller. When this laborious work was finally completed, the Michigan officer was ready to announce his final judgment. He advised the St. Paul investigators that beyond doubt the anonymous telephone call had been made by the woman under suspicion.

It was now October 30, more than five months since the killing of Officer Sackett, and the time for decisive police action had come. A warrant charging Constance Louise Trimble with murder was issued at the request of Captain Ernest Williams, and she was promptly arrested despite her continued pleas that she was innocent of both the telephone call and the killing.

Next day she appeared in municipal court, where her lawyer, engaged by a group of sympathetic friends, challenged the court's jurisdiction, contending that the warrant had been improperly issued and that her arrest was illegal.

While this matter was pending, the district attorney, seeking to expedite proceedings, summoned the grand jury, which returned an indictment charging murder in the first degree. An early trial was contemplated.

Connie Trimble and her attorney, however, had other plans. To the surprise of the authorities, they petitioned for a writ of habeas corpus on the grounds of unlawful arrest. This was promptly denied by the municipal judge and an appeal was taken. Now, legalistically speaking, the fat was in the fire. The hearing before the appellate court would be far-reaching, testing not only the legality of the surreptitious circumstances under which the defendant's voice had been recorded but the admissibility of the evidence produced by Lieutenant Nash. It was an involved legal issue that never before had reached a Minnesota court.

The appeal hearing set a precedent in Minnesota, as three recognized experts in the science of acoustics and speech forensics became pivotal witnesses for the defense. Testifying for the state in support of the reliability of Voiceprints were Lieutenant Nash and Dr. Oscar Tosi. Tosi's scientific testimony had followed Nash's own recital of the means by which he had reached his conclusions and his own reliance on the accuracy of Voiceprint identification.

Hours were spent in Nash's examination by the state. A few excerpts from the record disclose the positiveness of his statements.

Q. What is your opinion [as to the voice of the woman caller]?

A. In my opinion the voice of Constance Trimble and the voice that made the call that I received on tape on June 1, 1970, are one and the same and could be no other.

Q. What is your degree of certainty in your expression of this opinion?

A. Beyond any doubt.

Dr. Peter Ladefoged of Los Angeles, who appeared later as a defense expert, testified that he was still of the opinion that spectographic Voiceprint identification was too uncertain to be admitted as evidence in a trial, but he did agree that use of spectograms to corroborate an opinion formed from listening to the tapes would make the opinion more reliable.

The appellate court's judgment, handed down some time later, marked a complete defeat for the accused woman and a victory for Nash and Tosi. It was the first time that Voiceprint operators had been accepted by a court as "expert witnesses."

On other contested issues as well the decision set a precedent in determining vital controversial legal points, and for this reason the appeal on the habeas corpus petition gained importance equal to that of the actual murder trial that followed. Countering the appellant's claim that the arrest warrant was issued on insufficient evidence, the judges found "that evidence necessary to establish probable cause to justify the issuance of a warrant for arrest . . . need not be as convincing as evidence which will sustain a conviction."

Then, upholding the admissibility of Voiceprint identification and the fact that in this case a specimen of the defendant's voice was obtained surreptitiously, the judge wrote:

"Voiceprints or spectograms are admissible to corroborate voice identification by ear if proper foundation is laid establishing the expertise of one preparing the spectograms.

"Even though recording of appellant's voice was surreptitiously obtained without her knowledge or consent, there was no violation of constitutional or statutory rights so as to make its reception inadmissible so long as no attempt was made to use any privileged information thus obtained."

Typical of the court's thoughtful reasoning in reaching its decision is this paragraph:

"It would seem to follow that if identification can be made by comparing a voice over a telephone or by requiring an accused to speak certain words in the presence of an accuser in a line-up or by means of other mechanical recording, the two tapes involved in this case, one of the voice of a known person and the other of an unknown, should be admissible for the purpose of comparison aurally, the same as if the words were spoken in some other manner, assuming that a foundation is laid showing that there has been no alteration of the tape and that the tape is mechanically perfected to the point where voices can be identified by it."

Another significant aspect of the lengthy opinion was that the judges gave recognition to the professional standing of Dr. Tosi and Lieutenant Nash, who testified for the state, and to Dr. Ladefoged, the defense expert. Referring to the pioneering work by Kersta and his associates, the judges agreed that "their experiments showed a remarkably high, 99.65 percent, success in identifying speakers by comparisons of Voiceprints."

With Connie Trimble's failure to squash the charges against her, the state moved fast to proceed with her trial for murder, and as the date approached, speculation mounted as to what course she would pursue. Many wondered how she and her counsel would counter the adverse court decision, yet in press interviews she still insisted, as she had so many times before, that she had not made the controversial telephone call and knew nothing about it.

Some believed that she would stand her ground, perhaps with faint hope that a jury might be favorable on the basis of reasonable doubt. At all events, a most unusual situation had developed and the press made the most of it.

Early in February, 1972, the case was called for trial in St. Paul and a jury was soon impaneled. The state's presentation in many ways was a repetition of the testimony given during the earlier habeas corpus hearing and its subsequent appeal. As had been expected, the anonymous telephone call and the wanton killing of Policeman Sackett were revealed to the jury in every detail. Nash and Tosi again told of their conclusions by Voiceprint comparisons.

At last the defense was called on to present its case. At once a strange silence fell over the crowded courtroom as listeners heard the words: "The defendant will please take the stand."

Connie Trimble, her face frozen, rose to her feet at the counsel table and walked haltingly to the witness chair. She raised a trembling hand to swear that she would tell "the truth and nothing but the truth"; then she took her seat, her eyes turned toward the ceiling.

After the usual perfunctory questions concerning her age, former place of residence, and her welfare status, her attorney blurted his key question:

"Did you or did you not make the anonymous telephone call to the police about which you have heard?"

For seconds she did not answer as she sat nervously twisting her handkerchief. No doubt she was weighing for the last time in her troubled mind the momentous question and the decision she already had reached. At this moment she must gamble for her freedom, asking herself which would more likely open prison doors—truth or falsehood. There were split seconds left to make a final choice.

Only the ticking of the courtroom clock was audible as the frightened young woman sat silently, the cynosure of all eyes.

Once more her lawyer repeated the question, louder this time, and those who heard it detected a note of impatience. Then suddenly, looking up, Connie Trimble in a whisper spoke the words that she hoped might move the scales in her favor.

"Yes sir, I did," she said at last.

Facing prison for a murder, she had carefully considered at last the powerful impact of Voiceprint testimony on her own precarious position and had concluded to tell the truth. There was a gambler's chance that the jury might believe her and be influenced by her frank statement of mitigating circumstances.

Responding to long, sharp questioning by her attorney, she insisted that in sending the police on the fatal mission she had absolutely no knowledge of a plot to fatally shoot an officer from ambush.

Actually, she swore, she had been duped into making the false call by two militant associates who had not disclosed their murderous purpose.

They had lied to her, she declared, with a story that they wished to meet policemen alone in an isolated place to discuss serious racial problems in the neighborhood that they believed could be solved only by secret dialogue rather than by a meeting with higher officials at headquarters.

It was a ruse, she testified, that she naïvely and stupidly accepted without thought of its real purpose or its consequences.

"And would you have made the call if you had realized its true purpose and what the result would be?" her lawyer pressed.

"Certainly not," she answered firmly. "Never in God's world."

With these words she cast a sly glance at the jurors, wondering how they would accept her confession. Their faces were frozen.

Over and over defense counsel hurled the same questions but with changed words, hoping to impress the jury with the reasonableness of his client's story.

When it was finally over, Connie Trimble stepped down from the witness chair. Soon she would know whether she had gambled wisely, but at least, she thought, her conscience would be clear.

The case of the defense, brief as it was, soon neared its close. There remained only the testimony of a handful of character witnesses, testifying that the accused never before had been in trouble with the law.

With the start of closing arguments the prosecutor bitterly attacked the defendant's admissions, emphasizing her earlier lies to the police and insisting that she was finally compelled to admit the truth only because Voiceprints had trapped her. He declared that, contrary to her testimony, she was still trying to protect the murderer. He closed with the statement that he was confident that intelligent jurors would understand the real meaning of defense tactics.

The defense pictured Connie Trimble as a gullible young woman who had acted thoughtlessly and stupidly for someone she trusted.

The jury finally retired, the defendant's fate in its hands. People lingered in the courtroom expecting a quick verdict that perhaps would mean a life sentence to prison, for Minnesota long since had abolished the death penalty.

The verdict, however, was not quick in coming. Hours passed before a knock on the door of the jury room summoned a bailiff. With no revealing expressions on their faces, the jurors returned to their places. The foreman handed a slip of paper to the clerk and silent spectators waited anxiously for the verdict.

"We, the jury," intoned the clerk, "find the defendant, Constance Louise Trimble, not guilty of murder in the first degree."

Connie heard the words and collapsed in her chair. Moments later she was surrounded by a host of friends, delighted but no doubt surprised at the outcome, which almost everyone agreed would have been different but for the impact of Voiceprint evidence.

Jurors later explained that in their opinions the state had not convinced them that the defendant had knowingly played a role in Officer Sackett's murder or that she knew anything of the real purpose of the disputed telephone call to the police.

A spokesman for the Ramsey County District Attorney's Office later added this comment:

"We think that the Voiceprint aspect of the case was completely vindicated in that she [Connie Trimble] admitted it was, in fact, she who made the phone call, as we contended by our proof with regard to the Voiceprints."

Soon after the verdict Miss Trimble regained her freedom. Ready to pick up the threads of a torn life, she went to live with relatives in another state. The killer or killers of the policemen were never apprehended, having presumably fled far from Minnesota.

Ironically, Connie's paramour, who had fathered her little girl, was sent to Nebraska State Penitentiary some time later to serve thirty-five years for a bank holdup in which a policeman was wounded.

XIV

The "Cuban Mafia's" Extortion Plot

The extortioner identified himself as a member of the "Cuban Mafia."

Whether he represented such an organization or was aciting only for himself remains a mystery. The significant fact is that he was outwitted by Voiceprints, and a criminal career was aborted soon after it had started.

The case took place in Miami, Florida, in the spring of 1970, when seventy-year-old Joaquin B. Cortez suddenly found himself the target for a series of demands for payment of $1,000 under penalty of serious harm to himself and his family.

The first, scrawled on a postcard with the "Mafia" signature, left Cortez terrified, for he knew that some of his countrymen, all of them Spanish, had suffered violence when they resisted such calls for money. Nevertheless, he decided not to complain to the authorities at this time, fearing that police action might further jeopardize him and his family.

For the next few days he remained cautiously on his guard, praying that nothing more sinister would occur, but his hopes soon vanished. At his home he received threatening telephone calls and he knew at once that he was really in trouble. A man identifying himself as Guillermo Pantoja, speaking in Spanish, renewed the demand and repeated the same menacing phrases.

This time Cortez called on the police and related what had occurred. Sergeant Vince Oller of the Dade County Public Safety Department, a shrewd investigator with many contacts in the Spanish and Cuban communities, was put in charge of the case and the victim was promised all possible protection.

Oller, knowing from experience that extortioners are usually relentless, went first to Cortez' home and installed a recording device on the telephone so that any further demands could be taped. He was not disappointed, because the calls continued in rapid succession—on April 28, May 2, and May 6. The voice was always the same and there was little if any difference in what was said, excepting that in the last message specific instructions were given for payment of the money. This had been overheard by Sergeant Oller, who was in the Cortez home at the time and was listening over an extension line.

Cortez was told that on May 9, three days later, he should place the money in a shoebox, deliver it to the Ferrolana Grocery, and tell the grocer that a "Mr. Pantoja" would pick it up before dark.

The sergeant, after conferring with his superiors, planned to set a trap. Instructions were carefully followed on the designated day, but instead of putting the entire amount in the box, $40 in greenbacks were placed over layers of crumpled newspapers which were sprayed with fluorescent dust to obtain fingerprints of the extortioner or his accomplices.

The box was delivered by Cortez himself as directed, and the grocer, José Perez, was requested to give it to a "Mr. Pantoja."

Less than an hour later Perez answered the telephone in his store. A man introducing himself as "Mr. Pantoja" inquired whether a parcel had been left there for him and on receiving an affirmative reply he advised that someone would call there shortly to pick it up.

When this word was relayed to Oller, posted close to the store, he immediately signaled to three plainclothesmen seated in a car parked in a spot well concealed from the view of anyone in or near the grocery. They, with the sergeant, were to close in quickly on whoever was seen leaving with the bundle.

They did not have long to wait. Soon afterward a heavyset man and a boy were seen dashing for a parked car, the younger one holding the package under his arm. Moments later they were speeding away.

The unmarked police car gave chase at once, as cries to halt went unheeded. The pursuit continued for several blocks as the officers, hindered by heavy traffic, slowly gained on their quarry.

They were zig-zagging from one street to another when suddenly an arm was thrust through the open window of the car ahead and the package fell to the ground.

Minutes later the fugitives' car was forced to the curb by a quick police maneuver and the occupants were ordered to put up their hands. The boy identified himself as Joseph Miguel Alea and said he was nineteen years of age. The other gave his name as Alfredo Campa. Both were Cubans speaking Spanish, which Oller spoke fluently, but his questioning of the pair was to no avail, because both men stubbornly refused to respond or to make any statement.

The boy finally admitted, however, that he was a son of José Bruno Alea. The two were then told by Oller that they would be driven to the father's home for an explanation.

The senior Alea stared at his son and the others with surprise and demanded to know the reason for their presence. Oller and his companion, Officer Rafael Aguirre, reported what had occurred, but the father merely shrugged his shoulders and said he knew nothing of his boy's affairs.

As he continued talking, a strange feeling came over Oller. "I seem to have heard that voice before," the officer told himself. "It's familiar, but where have I heard it?" And then, quite suddenly, he remembered. It sounded very much like the voice he had heard over Cortez' telephone, but he could not be positive.

He pressed for further conversation and suspicion gradually turned to certainty. He then called on Officer Aguirre to guard the three while he went for something in the police car. His real purpose was to "bug" the police car.

Returning to the house, he announced that the trio would be taken to headquarters, and on the way the elder Alea was questioned continuously while the hidden machine recorded every word of a rambling conversation in which the father repeatedly denied ever having telephoned the victim, but he did say that Cortez owed him $1,000 following a business deal. This, he insisted, was in no way connected with the threats Cortez had received.

Further grilling at the station being to no avail, Campa and young Alea were booked on charges of conspiracy to commit extortion. Hours later they were free on bail.

Meanwhile the discarded package, which had been picked up by the officers, was carefully examined in the police laboratory. The wrapping paper bore marks of the fluorescent powder and there were traces of it on Campa's hands. This evidence was put away for use at the trial.

The question of the senior Alea's involvement puzzled the authorities. It seemed obvious that the two in custody had acted under orders, yet there was practically no evidence against the older man beyond Oller's identification of the voice. This, of course, would be checked by Voiceprints, but even then some corroboration would probably be needed.

In the ensuing weeks detectives interviewed relatives and friends of José Bruno Alea. All were tight-lipped and only a few would even admit knowing the man.

These efforts might have ended in failure but for an unforeseen circumstance. José Bruno was arrested on a charge of violating a building code. It was then that Oller, turning his inquiry to this direction, discovered that Alea was in serious financial difficulties and had been trying desperately to raise money, a possible reason for extortion. And then, suddenly, the accused father disappeared.

This led to orders for a citywide search and while this was under way it was decided to turn to Voiceprint tests.

The burden fell on Lieutenant Nash and Dr. Tosi, to whom recordings of the threatening telephone calls were sent together with 2,600 feet of magnetic tape carrying the senior

Alea's conversation in Spanish during the car ride to headquarters on the day that the other two had been arrested.

For Nash this presented a serious challenge, since he did not speak a word of Spanish and had never before been called on to study spectograms made from a foreign language. But with his experience in Voiceprint techniques he knew that somehow he could find a way. After much thought and many experiments, he finally reasoned that if he could not compare the images of words on spectograms, he could at least check sounds with effective and accurate results.

In Michigan his colleague, Dr. Tosi, already had made aural comparisons of the voices and had found them to be exactly the same. This, of course, was only preliminary to Nash's work in converting the tapes into spectograms to see whether they would corroborate Tosi's findings.

Nash finally overcame his difficulty by engaging a student fluent in Spanish as an aide. This man first listened to the tapes to catch the sounds of syllables and words, then relayed the sounds to Nash, who painstakingly linked them to the delicate lines of the spectograms. It was a difficult task, for in addition to the language problem, Nash was obliged to work with 2,600 feet of tape, any portion of which might provide a vital clue.

Pursuing this course, Nash became fully convinced that the telephone recorded messages and the known voice of José Bruno Alea were identical beyond the slightest doubt. In other words, Alea was in fact the mysterious "Mr. Pantoja."

His conclusions were sent to Sergeant Oller and his colleagues in Miami, giving them the specific evidence that they required. But the elder Alea was still missing.

The search was accelerated and extended over other states, with a description of the wanted man broadcast by teletype, airmail, and posted circulars.

Not until several months later did word come that the hunt was over—Alea had been arrested in Chicago. He was returned to Florida to face trial for extortion.

With his son and Campa, already similarly charged, he appeared before Judge Jack M. Turner in Criminal Court of

Dade County, who would decide the case himself, the defendants having waived a jury trial.

Voiceprints were to be the basis of the prosecution's case. Dr. Tosi, one of the first witnesses called, laid the foundation for Nash's testimony, the procedure he had followed in many other cases. He began by testifying that Voiceprints were an accurate and useful tool in criminal investigations. A student of Spanish, he told the court, as he had previously advised the police, that checking only by ear he had recognized the voice of the man calling himself Pantoja as that of the elder Alea.

Nash, next to take the stand, gave a detailed account of his study of the spectograms and how, working for the first time with a foreign language, he had reached the same definite conclusions as his colleague.

In their own defense, the three accused men vigorously denied any wrongdoing, insisting that they were in no way involved in the "Mafia" extortion plot.

Now it was up to Judge Turner to make his own decision and he did not hesitate in finding the three defendants guilty. José Bruno Alea, judged by the court to have been the prime mover in the extortion, was sentenced to serve one year in prison. The others were given similar terms, but with the provision that they would be released on two years' probation after serving thirty days in jail.

The elder Alea resented his conviction and announced that he would appeal. He and his counsel insisted that the trial judge had erred in permitting the introduction of Voiceprint evidence since at no time in the state's legal history had this been accepted by any court.

To this the appellate court took strong exception. It cited an earlier ruling of the State Supreme Court upholding the admissibility of testimony relating to aural voice comparisons, though at that time Voiceprints were not a factor. In that case the high court held that "testimony is admissible to establish the identity of an accused even by one having heard his voice, and such evidence is not to be considered as circumstantial but as direct and positive proof of a fact, and its probative value is a question for the jury."

Referring then to the case at bar, the court, after citing decisions in other courts supportive of Voiceprints, found that "the evidentiary value of the Voiceprints, and therefore of the experts' testimony, was properly submitted to the trier of fact."

Alea's appeal was denied and Florida joined the ranks of other states accepting Voiceprints as legal evidence.

XV

When Loan Sharks Bite

The meeting was a routine monthly gathering of a journalism society in New Jersey.

The invited guest was a young, little-known assistant attorney general, and those who came expected an informal, innocuous address on relations between the press and law-enforcement agencies. Instead a bombshell exploded and another case of extortion came to light.

To the surprise of everyone, the speaker opened a Pandora's box. Out of it came a scandal that shook the state for months. It reached into the state house, the legislature, and the courts. When it was over, political heads had fallen after a three-pronged official inquiry conducted separately by a legislative committee, a special grand jury, and the ethical conduct committee of the supreme court.

Highlighting the climax was the introduction of Voiceprints that provided an ending differing from public opinion and a jury verdict that few had foreseen.

The provocative speaker was William J. Brennan III, a son of a Justice of the United States Supreme Court.

At the start of the meeting Brennan launched at once into startling charges of extortion and corruption in the state legislature. Asserting boldly that certain of its members were "too comfortable" with leaders of organized crime, he pointed an accusing finger at a prominent legislator, declaring that he and two influential lawyers had taken part in an unsavory out-of-court settlement of an extortion case. Even participation of Mafia characters in state affairs did not escape his mention.

Scarcely had the meeting ended when word reached the newspapers, and reporters began delving into what had been dubbed "the loan shark case," an issue between a businessman heavily in debt and a money lender that had been dropped abruptly when the merchant refused to testify before the grand jury regarding a menacing death threat for which he previously had blamed the other. The threat, he had charged, followed his sudden refusal to continue making allegedly usurious payments on two loans. Although Brennan did not say so at the time, he implied that the debtor had been "bought off."

The explosive address, given before the New Jersey Chapter of Sigma Delta Chi, took place on an evening in mid-December, 1968, and though much time has passed, it continues to be a subject of reflective discussion and marks a significant victory for Kersta's Voiceprints.

The startling repercussions from the lawyer's speech far transcended the importance of the specific case, no doubt because public opinion had turned sharply against loan sharks in the wake of exposés in which some of their victims, although brutally beaten, had refused to press charges for fear of reprisals.

The principals in the case referred to by Brennan were virtually unknown outside of their own little circles. Yet, when finis was finally written to the scandal, three prominent lawyers, one of them a member of the state legislature, and another a legal official of his community, faced suspension from professional practice. Others scurried for cover and two disappeared.

The little-known principals in the early legal controversy were John DiGilio, a thirty-nine-year-old former professional boxer, of Jersey City, who had also been a boatman aboard a tug; and Julius Pereria Jr., chairman of the Middlesex County Young Democrats, who operated the DuRite Car Wash in Woodbridge, a sprawling town in the metropolitan area that has grown to more than 100,000 since World War II.

Because of the many ramifications developing in rapid-fire succession following Brennan's speech, the story can best be told chronologically, disclosing how one development led to another. Only a short time after the fraternity meeting and its exciting disclosures, Edward J. Dolan, prosecutor for Middlesex County in New Jersey, sat behind closed doors with a hastily summoned investigating committee of the legislature, relating what he had learned about the manner in which a grand jury inquiry into Pereria's accusations against DiGilio had ended some time before.

He explained that Pereria had borrowed $1,000 on two occasions—the first in 1966, the second a year later—from DiGilio, a heavily built man five feet eight inches tall, agreeing to pay $50 a week interest until he would be able to repay the principal. Despite business reverses the borrower had continued the weekly payments until he had paid a total of $7,400. Then, deciding that he already had paid far too much, he informed DiGilio that there would be no more checks. The other flew into a rage and walked away.

Not long afterward, according to Dolan's recital, Pereria had received a telephone call at his place of business from a man who said, "I'll come down there and chop your . . . head off."

Badly frightened, Pereria went to the police insisting that the voice was that of DiGilio, which he said he recognized by a peculiar raspy note that contrasted with a rather high tone. It was then August, 1968.

Charges were preferred against DiGilio, but when the case was called before Judge Samuel Sladkus in Woodbridge Municipal Court the plaintiff flatly refused to testify. The matter was turned over to the grand jury and again Pereria remained silent. The grand jury, finding its hands tied, returned a "no bill," which meant that the matter was ended.

Dolan, in reporting these facts, asserted that he knew there had been an out-of-court settlement; in other words the accuser had been "paid off." He promised to provide further details at a later time or at the conclusion of a grand jury hearing that already had been started.

With two separate inquiries under way, Dolan pressed hard for grand jury action. Pereria was summoned and this time he was ready to talk. He told of the threats which he swore had come from DiGilio, adding that three mobsters sent to his car wash business by DiGilio had broken in and damaged it.

The result was an indictment accusing both DiGilio and an associate, fifty-eight-year-old Gerald Grimaldi, of conspiracy in threats and extortion against Pereria. Grimaldi, it was alleged, had introduced the other two; he also had been identified as one of the trio at the car wash.

What Pereria had to tell about the settlement that previously had silenced him became one of many sensations at the trial of DiGilio, which opened on February 4, 1970, in New Brunswick, the county seat of Middlesex.

Its setting was a study in sharp contrasts. While the nature of the case was grim and forbidding, it was to be aired in a colorful, modernly furnished courtroom on the third floor of the relatively new county courthouse, a five-story structure overlooking a century-old county jail.

Judge John B. Melineux, who was to preside, had earlier ordered separate trials for the two defendants, since Grimaldi had suffered a severe heart attack. It was the first of many delays.

Even before questioning of prospective jurors began, Voiceprints became the subject of bitter argument. Defense Attorney Michael Querques had moved for permission to have Lawrence Kersta compare a tape of DiGilio's voice with a recording made by Pereria at his business place when he received the threatening phone call. His request met with heated opposition from J. Norris Harding, the assistant prosecutor, who accused his opponent of "trying to shift the burden of the defense to the state."

The court reserved judgment, at the same time ordering a day's postponement to allow counsel to go to Grand Bahama Island, where the defense claimed it would establish that DiGilio was with others at the time of the phone threat and that no call had gone from the island to New Jersey on that day.

The defendant's contention was fully verified. DiGilio had scored his first important point.

With resumption of the trial, Voiceprints again became a controversial issue. The court, first having refused to order the state to give the defense recordings of the threatening message, later relented but reserved the right to bar such evidence. This was based on the fact that the state's high court had not yet ruled on this new type of evidence.

No sooner had this been disposed of than other delays became necessary. During an afternoon recess DiGilio had fallen overboard from a tug, sustaining painful injuries. There was a squabble over the long postponement demanded by the defense, and the court finally agreed on a two-day recess which later was extended after the defendant was hurt again in an automobile crash.

After still further postponements DiGilio finally returned to court on February 24, and in a short time a jury of seven men and an equal number of women was impaneled.

Harding, the prosecutor, in his opening statement, reviewed the details of the loan transaction, explaining that Pereria had met the defendant through the latter's friend, Grimaldi, then owner of a Woodbridge paint store. He went still further, and for the first time details of the cash settlement that sealed the accuser's lips went officially into the record.

Harding told the jury that Attorney David Friedland, a member of the State Assembly and its minority leader, had represented DiGilio in negotiating the settlement with Pereria's lawyer, Norman Robbins, law director of Woodbridge Township. Through their agreement, the prosecutor stated, DiGilio had paid $6,500 to his creditor and the matter was considered closed.

DiGilio's attorney, Querques, was on his feet interrupting. He implied that the money had been paid by the lender in good faith "for his own peace of mind" and because he did not wish to worry his pregnant wife.

After the prosecutor had concluded, Pereria was called to the stand as the state's key witness. Obviously nervous, he related the details of the loan and his difficulty in meeting the weekly payments. "I knew it was shy money," he testified. "I knew the general procedures. If you don't pay, you end up with threats or wind up with your head busted." He even related a conversation with Grimaldi when they discussed the possibility of having the car wash set afire for the insurance.

A titter ran through the courtroom when the witness testified that the New Jersey police "wired me for sound," referring to a microphone that detectives had secreted in his clothing to obtain recordings of his conversations with Grimaldi, who often reminded him of the dire consequences that might follow his refusal to continue payments.

These tapes, liberally laced with four-letter words, were later read in open court. Spectators had a field day.

Soon afterward the much-talked-of pay-back by DiGilio to Pereria at last became a part of the official court record. The details were disclosed by Assemblyman Friedland, a young man with thick brown hair and long sideburns, who appeared in an Edwardian gray suit, eager to tell what he knew. With him, as a corroborating witness, was Robbins.

After picturing DiGilio as a troubled man, whose pregnant wife had undergone spinal surgery, Friedland stated that the defendant had paid $6,500 to Pereria, following arrangements that he said had been concluded on the floor of the legislature after a series of conferences in which Pereria's demand for a larger sum was finally reduced to the accepted figure. The witness admitted that he had told DiGilio of the possible danger of a civil suit over charges of usury, although others had assured him that he was certain of acquittal on the pending accusations.

In closing, the defense lawyer insisted that his client was innocent of any wrongdoing and had agreed to the payment rather than endure the strain of a trial because of his wife's illness.

Robbins followed him to the stand with his own version of the money transaction. He said that he had received $1,000 for his services.

During cross-examination of the two lawyer-witnesses strange names flitted in and out of the testimony. There was mention of "The Moose," of "John the Greek," and others, but their real identities were not disclosed, though their sobriquets added interest to the courtroom drama.

The defense scored heavily when it opened its case on the morning of March 5. As had been expected, its first witness, Nicholas Vaccaro, testified that he had been with DiGilio and the latter's wife on a four-day gambling junket to Grand Bahama Island off the Florida coast and that they were all together there on the day that the defendant was accused of making the threatening call to New Jersey. To prove his story, he showed the jury photographs of the party at the island casino.

Then, on the following day, came the dramatic climax of the trial—Voiceprint evidence. While it had been rumored that the defense had "something scientific up its sleeve," the appearance of Dr. Tosi came as a complete surprise. Word that something unusual was to happen resulted in a packed courtroom.

"Who's he?" one spectator asked another as the bearded professor, responding to his name, walked briskly to the witness chair.

"The Voiceprint man," someone whispered; and another, catching the words, followed with: "Voiceprints, what's that?" They were soon to know.

After Tosi had been sworn and asked about his qualifications, he related that he had received the tape recordings from the defense and had compared the spectograms produced from them.

"Now, Dr. Tosi, what are your conclusions?" asked Attorney Querques in DiGilio's behalf.

Tosi's reply caused an excited stir among the spectators. Testifying under oath, he declared that the voices were not the same—in other words, Voiceprints had established that DiGilio was *not* the man who made the death threats against Pereria.

To further emphasize the impact of the expert's judgment, defense counsel asked the court's permission to provide a demonstration. DiGilio read aloud from a transcript of one conversation, playing the role of the extortioner; Detective Captain Silvio Donatelli took Pereria's part. When they had finished Dr. Tosi looked at the judge repeating what he had said before: "The two voices belong to two different persons."

To support the Michigan scientist, the defense called a second expert, Dr. Louis J. Gerstman, a psychology professor and speech researcher from New York University, who also had studied the tapes.

"The same voice," he declared, "could not possibly have made the two recordings. I am certain that these are the voices of two different people." DiGilio, he went on to explain, "is a tenor while the man who called Pereria had a considerably lower voice."

The defense now had dealt telling blows to the state's case, but it still had not finished. "And now," Attorney Querques announced, "we will hear from the expert who invented Voiceprints. Mr. Kersta, will you please come forward?"

Necks were craned as the tall, lanky engineer with a gray Van Dyke, walked rapidly down the aisle. He was first asked by the judge, as had been inquired of the others, whether his testimony would support the defense, for New Jersey was not yet ready to admit such evidence by the prosecution. After assuring the judge that he was appearing in the defendant's behalf, he proceeded with the usual self-qualifying statements. Then, laying a foundation for the all-important question he was expecting, Kersta told how he had made spectograms of the recordings and had compared them.

"And just what did you find?" the lawyer pressed.

"The unknown voice was not the voice of Mr. DiGilio," he replied.

Under cross-examination he did not conceal his anger when Harding, the prosecutor, tried to confuse him with a question. Having personally been to the New Jersey laboratory with a detective, Harding had come away with seven spectograms and now he asked the witness how many voices they represented.

Kersta bristled. "I will not jeopardize a scientific technique," he retorted, "by attempting to read these graphs while I'm on the witness stand. I don't perform before an audience."

The question went unanswered.

The jury was informed that each of the experts had reached his conclusion by slightly different methods of comparisons.

The climax of the trial was over, but the defense still had more to say. It called Grimaldi, awaiting trial on similar charges, and he added more confusion to the already complicated case. His version was that actually the loans had been made by him rather than by DiGilio; that therefore the defendant would have had no reason to threaten Pereria.

DiGilio's appearance on the stand as his own witness marked the approaching end of the trial. He denied making the threatening call or ever having loaned money to his accuser. Asked why, then, he had agreed to a $6,500 payment to Pereria, he answered, "I was buying peace of mind." It was his way of explaining that he feared his wife would suffer a breakdown if he were compelled to face a jury trial. "She was crying all the time," he told the jury. "She was driving me crazy." And, recalling his arrest, he added: "I'm sitting in the jail wondering what I done. After a while a detective told me of the charges and I told him 'Impossible—you picked the wrong guy.'"

Harding in cross-examination drew a few laughs as he pressed the witness for some explanation as to why Pereria had singled him out for an allegedly false accusation. DiGilio thought for a moment before replying: "This guy took a million-to-one shot and picked me."

"Picked you out of a hat?" the prosecutor inquired, smiling.

"I don't know," he answered, "but I'm here."

Mrs. Ellen DiGilio, following her husband to the stand, did her best to corroborate his explanation of why he agreed to a cash settlement to stay prosecution. She referred to her highly nervous condition over his troubles, adding that they both were afraid that their child might be born dead, as her doctor had feared. She also disclosed that her husband's income from two jobs had totaled $27,728 the previous year, a point that neither side chose to pursue.

Near the close of its case the defense scored again through the testimony of other witnesses who said that they had been gambling with DiGilio and his wife on Grand Bahama Island on the day of the threatening call to Pereria.

Harding's rebuttal for the state was brief, but some courtroom attendants believed it indicated his fear of the Voiceprint testimony in the defense's behalf. Again referring to his visit to Kersta's laboratory, he related that he had been given a few spectograms to illustrate the method; then in derisive tones he told the court that "one looks like a mountain and the other like a tree." It was obvious that he was trying to discredit the testimony of Kersta and his colleagues.

Closing arguments provided an interesting study in forensic styles. Querques, at times highly emotional, painted a touching word picture of DiGilio and his wife, suffering mental anguish as they awaited the birth of their child. He emphasized the findings of the Voiceprint experts who had testified for the defense, stressing his claim that a man proved innocent by science had been brought to trial. Sometimes there were tears in his eyes; occasionally he shouted to impress the jury. Now and then he lowered his voice to a whisper.

Harding, on the other hand, spoke calmly and with no emotion. In his direct fashion he reviewed the state's case, attempting to place DiGilio in the center of a web of incriminating evidence and he branded Querques' plea for sympathy as "one grand hoax."

Judge Melineux gave his instructions and the jurors retired. It was March 12, 1970, a few days less than two years after Brennan's sensational speech. Taking of testimony had consumed ten and a half days.

Speculation was rife over the outcome, though many left the courtroom expecting long deliberations. Some believed that the Voiceprint evidence had clinched the case for the defense; others questioned whether "the new-fangled machine," as they called it, would influence the jury. And there were those who believed that it would be impossible to reach a verdict in view of the complicated and conflicting evidence involved. At best the result appeared to be anybody's guess, yet no one had imagined the speed with which DiGilio's fate would be determined.

The clock showed the passage of only seventy minutes since the jurors had retired when there came a knock on the jury-room door. Judge Melineux was hastily summoned, court was convened, and the bailiff rapped for order.

DiGilio, in a chair beside his lawyer, sat rigidly as the usual formalities received necessary attention. Not far away his accuser, Pereria, flanked the prosecutor at the state's table.

The jurors were escorted back to the box, their faces immobile, with no indication of their decision. The foreman rose and at the court's request read the writing on the slip of paper in his hand.

As he spoke the words "not guilty," applause broke out among those remaining in the courtroom. DiGilio's face beamed as he moved toward his wife, whose tears stained her makeup. They walked outside arm in arm and to newsmen DiGilio declared: "I feel twenty years younger. I was never this nervous before a fight." Then he asked his wife to phone his mother. "I'm even too nervous to do that," said the former boxer.

Later in the day Kersta and his associates received the news. They were gratified that the jury had accepted their interpretation of Voiceprint evidence.

However, the old scandal that Brennan had exposed long before had not yet reached a final conclusion. During the progress of the trial a special legislative committee had conducted an intensive inquiry to determine whether the three prominent lawyers involved in DiGilio's repayment of borrowed money and interest to Pereria were guilty of unethical conduct. At its conclusion the New Jersey Supreme Court directed that the trio be summoned to a hearing in their own defense.

When this was over the high court ordered the three men suspended from practice—Friedland and Robbins for six months each; Querques for three months.

There now remained only the case of Gerald Grimaldi, once DiGilio's co-defendant, his trial having been separated from the other because of illness. Though it had been intended to begin his trial with as little delay as possible, more technicalities were raised; then Grimaldi became sick again.

The matter dragged on for more than a year until July, 1972, when Grimaldi suddenly waived trial and pleaded guilty to taking part in a conspiracy to threaten Pereria. He was sentenced to serve from one to two years in New Jersey state prison and fined $1,000 by Superior Court Judge Charles M. Morris, Jr. It was an ironic turn in the long-lingering case that would have been dropped and forgotten but for Attorney Brennan's speech to a fraternity more than three years before.

The identity of the man who actually threatened Pereria over the telephone still remains a mystery that Voiceprints cannot solve.

XVI

A Double Dilemma

In the early winter of 1972 two men holding important public offices in New Jersey's criminal justice system faced serious dilemmas. Though each struggled with a different type of problem, Voiceprints were the basis of their concern.

John J. Pribish, assistant prosecutor of Middlesex County, was fighting desperately to convict two men on trial for extortion and making threats against a man's life, but their terrified accuser flatly refused to testify despite continued warnings of a jail sentence for contempt. Pribish realized that without Voiceprint evidence he would lose his case.

The other man was Municipal Judge John B. Melineux of New Brunswick, who had been called on by the State Supreme Court to decide whether or not to admit such testimony by the prosecution rather than the defense for the first time in the state's legal history.

No wonder, then, that each man in his own way felt the weight of his responsibility. And Voiceprint experts who had testified for hours under both direct- and cross-examination, waited anxiously for the outcome. In many ways the case was as complicated as it was dramatic and unique. It occupied the attention of police, the FBI and the courts for more than five years while opposing counsel battled over legal technicalities and the accuracy of Voiceprints.

In some respects the legal controversy bore similarities to

the DiGilio trial, for the state's concern over so-called loan shark practices was involved. The locale was the same, yet in other ways the issues and the outcome were far different. There were no political ramifications, as in the other case, but a defense lawyer who had argued vigorously for Voiceprints in DiGilio's behalf opposed them in this court battle.

The charges involved first came to official attention in 1967 when forty-eight-year-old Albert Soffer of Edison, New Jersey, walked into police headquarters in New Brunswick pleading for protection for himself, his wife, and family. He described himself as a used-car salesman in Woodbridge, with a penchant for gambling that kept him constantly in debt. Sharply dressed, he looked more like a race-track habitué than a businessman, and he spoke in the language of his avocation.

Soffer explained that because he was unable to continue payments of a $7,400 debt he had been viciously assaulted and later threatened with further injury or even death.

He accused two men: Armand Faugno of Englewood Cliffs, owner of a trucking company and an alleged loan shark; and the latter's reputed "muscleman," Thomas Angelo Andretta of Hasbrouck Heights. Apparently eager to disclose all of his troubles, Soffer answered many questions asked by three detectives who were to play important roles in the lengthy procedures that followed. They were Captain Silvio Donatelli, Joseph de Marino, senior investigator for the public defender, and Captain Howard A. True. To these officers Soffer explained that he first had borrowed $1,000 in 1961 from Faugno and had been forced to continue with loans until he owed the present $7,400 balance, on which he no longer could make the required payments.

This incensed both Faugno and Andretta to such an extent that their anger turned to violence, Soffer declared. In the first encounter, he stated, Andretta had punched him in the ribs, knocking him to the ground, and had menacingly displayed a switchblade knife to emphasize his demand that a payment be made within the next few days.

Soon afterward Soffer had telephoned Faugno to complain

of the assault and was bluntly told: "He should have stabbed you; you'll be in the hospital next." Further threats had followed.

At this point the detectives realized the need for corroborative evidence and their minds turned to Voiceprints. This, of course, would require recordings of the alleged threats, and Soffer was more than willing to cooperate. A tape machine was adjusted to the police station telephone, and while the officers listened, the man with the complaint called both of those he had accused and, according to the detectives, the threats were repeated in much the same words. Now they had some of the evidence they required, but samples of the known voices of the accused would be required. This would be an easy matter—or so they thought—not knowing then that years of acrimonious court proceedings lay ahead before they would be permitted to fully present what appeared to be an open-and-shut case.

The next step was a grand jury inquiry, which ended in the indictment of Faugno and Andretta after Soffer's testimony had been corroborated by the detectives. Faugno was arrested as he sat eating at his accustomed table in a restaurant near his place of business. Andretta surrendered a few days later. Both denied their guilt.

The first unexpected halt in the wheels of justice came abruptly when Soffer was called to the stand in Judge Melineux's court at what was to be the preliminary hearing of both defendants. Assistant Prosecutor John E. Bachman opened with his first question concerning the financial transactions that had led to the trouble. With sealed lips Soffer, stared at his interrogator and shook his head. "I refuse to answer" was all that he would say.

Bachman followed with another question and then a third. The response was the same. In all, twelve questions in quick succession brought the same result, though the plantiff finally explained that he was standing on constitutional rights guaranteed by the Fifth Amendment, which protects a person against self-incrimination. It was an answer that the state was unwilling to accept and its pertinence was not clear. Obviously, Soffer was fearful of retaliation, but he did not say so.

He was admonished by the court to think the matter over. The case was continued to the end of the month, but when the accuser and the accused came to court again, Soffer still declined to testify.

Faugno and Andretta, seated with their counsel, made no effort to conceal their delight. Both had assumed the air and dress of successful businessmen. Faugno, immaculate in gray clothes and heavy-rimmed eyeglasses; his colleague in a smart checkered coat with light slacks. They beamed when the prosecutor admitted to the court that he might be obliged to drop the case for lack of the plaintiff's testimony.

There was another long continuance due to crowded court calendars and the case moved into the following year, though the lapse of time had failed to bring about a change in Soffer's attitude.

At the next court session defense attorneys Michael Querques and Harvey Weissbard renewed their motion for dismissal, arguing that the matter had dragged on for close to two years. The request was denied and Judge Melineux announced that the accuser would be cited for contempt and sent to jail unless he changed his mind. It was finally agreed that the detectives would be permitted to testify as to their conversations with Soffer and the recordings they had made of the threats.

Defense lawyers were on their feet at once with objections. Long legal arguments ensued, with victory for the state. Two of the officers, de Marino and True, related not only what had been expected of them concerning the beating and the threats, but they retold what Soffer had said about the terms of the loans. He had originally borrowed $1,000 to be repaid at $100 a week for twelve weeks with the provision that if he missed a payment he would be charged 5 percent additional of the balance each week. Soffer had soon found himself in financial quicksand and was obliged to borrow additional sums with which to meet the terms of the original deal.

Mrs. Soffer testified as to what her husband had told her of his experiences. It was actually a recital of what he had previously refused to say in open court.

Again a long continuance was ordered. Lawyers for the

state speculated over the reasons for Soffer's stubborn silence. While he admitted that he feared for his own life and that of his family, various other reasons were advanced to explain his reliance on the Fifth Amendment. There appeared to be general agreement that he was fearful of becoming involved in tax trouble as well as the possibility of difficulty over what he regarded as discrepancies in some details which he had told the police.

December, 1971, was approaching and responsibility for prosecuting the case had been transferred to Pribish, as supervising assistant prosecutor of Middlesex County. It was not a simple burden to inherit.

Pribish, a skillful and resourceful lawyer, reviewed the matter from its inception. The more he studied it the more convinced he became that only two recourses lay between him and total defeat. One was the remote possibility that Soffer could be induced to testify; the other was the even more remote likelihood that Judge Melineux might permit the introduction of Voiceprints. In either case he faced tremendous barriers.

Soffer had repeated many times that he would go to jail for contempt rather than risk the danger of reprisals for telling his story in court. As to the chance of presenting Voiceprint evidence, Pribish knew that New Jersey law permitted such testimony only in defense of the accused; a high court previously had ruled against its use by the prosecution.

The prosecutor fully recognized his dilemma and faced it courageously. And when his final desperate efforts to induce the plaintiff to take the stand had completely failed, he turned to voice spectograms as his last chance, although the defense already had publicly made known its intention of fighting him every inch of the way.

Pribish's initial strategy was a motion calling upon the court to direct the two defendants to provide samples of their voices for comparison with the police recordings. And to lay the necessary foundation to support his plea, he knew that he must first convince the court that this new type of evidence was reliable, accurate, and scientifically acceptable. Over strenuous defense objections he summoned Dr. Tosi and Lieutenant Nash.

Obviously they could not be questioned then about the case at the bar; their testimony must be confined to only scientific judgments pertaining in a general way to the Voiceprint process.

Although almost every one of his questions was interrupted by objections, Pribish succeeded in getting into the record Tosi's testimony that the chances of error in Voiceprint use were practically nil. These statements, with accounts of the witness' own experience, were bolstered by Nash, who added that some of his spectogram decisions had been verified by confessions.

Both were subjected to vigorous cross-examination. In fact, Tosi sat in the witness chair for over seven hours, answering volley after volley of questions by the defense which futilely tried to discredit him as an expert and to belittle the value of the method.

As still further support of these two, Pribish summoned a third authority, Dr. Peter Ladefoged of Los Angeles, who had withdrawn his earlier criticism of the technique and now supported it.

The defense was quick in calling its own experts in rebuttal. From the Bell Laboratories in New Jersey it had called Dr. James L. Flanagan and Dr. Peter Danes, both of whom acknowledged that while the Voiceprint process had been developed beyond Kersta's initial work, it still had not advanced sufficiently to warrant its use in court as evidence.

After many days had been consumed in what some referred to as Pribish's "trial balloon," Judge Melineux brought the issue to a head in a twenty-page decision flatly banning the introduction of Voiceprint testimony, which meant that the defendants could not be required to provide voice samples. The court declared that the state had failed to produce sufficient evidence to justify a conclusion that the disputed method had received adequate acceptance in the scientific community. To lawyers and layman alike, it was apparent that he probably was also relying on New Jersey law permitting such testimony only to defend the accused, not prosecute him.

Pribish fully realized his predicament and the likelihood that the case was near collapse. An appeal to the higher court on the focal point appeared to be his only hope, for he knew now that he had only the testimony of the detectives to support the charges. Losing no time, he consulted Prosecutor John S. Kuththau, his superior, who authorized him to file notice of appeal without delay.

Meanwhile the trial proceeded on other elements of the case. Suddenly the FBI made an unexpected appearance. Called by the state, one of its agents, Robert J. Lally, related details of a previous raid by G-men on Faugno's place of business after undercover agents had tried to buy what were described as hijacked drugs worth in excess of a million dollars. Cards bearing Soffer's name had been found in Faugno's briefcase, evidence which the state held indicated loan-sharking operations.

This testimony, described by some as "a fishing expedition," was bitterly attacked by Defense Attorney Robert Lewandowski as "absolutely incredible," and the incident was dropped after the court had ordered FBI testimony stricken from the record, the raid and Faugno's arrest having occurred before Soffer's trouble had started.

The trial now marked time pending the supreme court's ruling on the state's appeal. Not until November 14, 1972, did that body render the decision that came as a complete surprise and a victory for the prosecution. Written by Justice Haydn Proctor, the ruling pointed out that since 1967 there had been increasing evidence in support of Voiceprints. Therefore the high court ruled unanimously that the two defendants were obliged to provide the voice samples demanded by the state for comparison purposes. The justices, however, ended their decision with a tremendous BUT. It would be for Judge Melineux and not for the justices to decide whether to admit the results of the Voiceprint tests in evidence. In simple language, the buck had been passed to the trial judge.

Pribish studied the opinion and regarded it as something of a semi-victory—a foot in the door. He reasoned that the supreme court, having recognized the expertise of the men testifying for the state, now had given favorable consideration to their opinions on the accuracy of Voiceprints as well as to the acceptance of such evidence in other states.

Of special concern to the prosecutor was the significance of the following paragraphs in the high court's findings:

"Our decision in this case to permit the Voiceprint test to be conducted while deferring final consideration of its admissibility is justified by both legal and practical considerations. If the experts provided by the state are not able to make a positive identification by the comparison of Voiceprints made by the defendants' voices with Voiceprints made from the tape recordings of the telephone conversations, the application of the state in this case for use of this kind of evidence will of course become moot. On the other hand, if the state's experts purport to be able to make a positive identification, the trial court will have the advantage of the proofs at the hearing directed above concerning the particular conditions which the test was actually conducted.

". . . Dr. Tosi indicated that there was an added potential for error when the recordings compared were as little as a month apart, although he was of the opinion that an even greater time lag would not necessarily make a vital difference. The present time lag will be over five years. In the abstract it is difficult to determine whether such an identification will be sufficiently reliable to be admissible. It is not clear that the time lag will produce a risk of error disadvantageous to the defendants; it may be that the lag will operate only to prevent an affirmative identification. We believe, however, that the trial judge will be aided in his task if he has detailed testimony from those persons with expertise in the use of this method concerning the potential for error of the scientific identification test under examination. In this case we think the state should at least be given the opportunity to conduct the test and then to sustain its burden of establishing that an identification of the defendants' voices (if any) arrived at is sufficiently reliable to be admissible at the trial for the jury's ultimate consideration."

Now it was Judge Melineux who faced a dilemma. He recognized that the supreme court had directed him to order the accused to provide voice samples for comparison. It also authorized him to use his own judgment whether or not to admit as evidence the results of that comparison. It was a weighty decision for any judge.

Accordingly he signed the first order directed by the supreme court justices. He specified that the defendants, in providing exemplars of their voices, should repeat some of the exact words that they were alleged to have used in the tape recordings obtained by the police over the telephone.

As it developed later, the phrases selected for this test, presumably because they were best suited for comparisons, included:

"Better [*obscenity*] do something . . . don't bother calling me. We ain't going to [*obscenity*]wait," and

"Would that be [*obscenity*] better . . . you know darn well . . ." There were several others.

However, while arrangements were being made for compliance with the court order, the judge decided to attempt once more, and for the last time, to induce Soffer to break his silence. The accuser was brought into court and directed to take the stand. When he again refused to testify the judge asked him to explain his position.

Soffer stared appealingly at the judge. "It's obvious why I'm not testifying," he stated in a loud, clear voice, "I'm scared for my family. I'd rather not jeopardize them. So if I have to go to jail, I'll go to jail."

Nothing more was said. Judge Melineux previously had intimated out of court that he was reluctant to order the man imprisoned under the circumstances. The case would have to stand or fall not only on the judgment of the Voiceprint experts but on the judge's ultimate decision as to the admissibility of the spectogram comparisons.

Court reconvened a few days later to hear the final decision of Tosi and Nash, who had subjected the Voiceprints to the customary tests and were ready to make known their findings. As one followed the other to the witness chair, the two testified that the voices were those of Faugno and Andretta. They swore that Andretta's voice appeared on the tape of the conversation with Soffer on March 22, 1967, and that Faugno had been the speaker in the call a day later.

Questioned sharply by Pribish, they testified that the time lapse of more than five years since the recordings taken by the police and those obtained long afterward under court order had no effect whatever on the test results.

Defense objections to the testimony of the experts, which had begun even before they took the stand, were resumed, even more aggressively, after they had presented their evidence.

Both attorneys, Querques and Lewandowski, bitterly criticized the scientific findings and the way in which they had been obtained. They charged, for example, that Tosi had concentrated his tests on similarities rather than dissimilarities.

Pressing their objections still further, they insisted that the time lapse involved in making the voice comparisons added materially to the chance of error, despite the testimony of the experts.

Nash, in response, stated that he had found no changes in his own voice over a five-year period and he cited a case tried in St. Louis where he had made an identification after a lapse of two years.

"How do you know you were right?" interjected Judge Melineux, referring to the St. Louis case.

"The person identified made a subsequent confession," Nash shot back.

The defense arguments continued, including the charge that their clients' constitutional rights had been violated.

The lawyers then requested a continuance to enable them to study copies of the incriminating graphs. Lewandowski told the judge that "I frankly feel that I do not see similarities but gross dissimilarities between the known and unknown voices." And Querques added that he intended to arrange the voice pictures into a chart which would be shown to the court in support of the defense position.

A continuance of a month was granted and the attorneys went to work.

When the case was called again on February 9, 1972, the defense came forward with a proposal of its own. Before presenting it, however, Querques again bitterly attacked the testimony of the experts, branding it as "scientifically worthless" and "a bunch of hocus-pocus."

Then, admitting that his new idea was his own, he

suggested that "the granddaddy" of the "invention," Lawrence Kersta, conduct the tests which would include samples of the ten or fifteen phrases spoken by the defendants at the court's direction. Querques went still further, stipulating that Judge Melineux and all of the lawyers in the case could be present to observe every step of Kersta's work.

Judge Melineux, who had been listening attentively, made no comment, but the proposal had brought Pribish quickly to his feet with strong objections. "Your offer comes too late," he declared. "I don't think it's a good thing." He added that the court now was obliged to rely on the expertise of Tosi and Nash, that it was for the judge to decide whether their testimony was truthful and credible, not whether he agreed with it.

The judge, obviously realizing that it was for him to decide the crux of the issue—to admit or ban the Voiceprint testimony —took the question under advisement. More time slipped by until he was ready to make known his decision. It came two weeks later, and newsmen, in reporting the historic occasion, commented that the jurist "has listened to more testimony about the validity of the Voiceprint technique than any other New Jersey judge and perhaps more than any judge in the country."

Before a crowded courtroom, tensely awaiting the ruling, Judge Melineux began with a fact-by-fact review of the issues involved. Men and women moved forward in their seats awaiting the final word that came at last—Voiceprint testimony would be admitted as evidence!

"The issue here to be resolved," the judge said, speaking slowly with careful choice of words, "cannot be disposed of without weighing the court's appraisal of the expert testimony of Dr. Tosi and Lieutenant Nash. . . .

"The court was impressed with their expertise and finds it to be reliable. Based upon this confidence, the court is of the opinion that the method is reliable in this case and therefore holds it to be admissible."

Judge Melineux had solved his dilemma as Pribish already had found an answer to his. Voiceprints had achieved another victory.

The second and final surprise came a month afterward, on

May 18, 1973, more than five years after the beginning of the case. Thomas Angelo Andretta confessed!

Standing before the bench, he announced that he had decided to waive trial and admitted his role as Faugno's "enforcer," the one who had threatened Soffer for failing to continue his loan payments. No one doubted that his decision to plead guilty had been motivated by the unprecedented decision of Judge Melineux to allow Voiceprint evidence.

His sentence disclosed a "bargain" made with the prosecutor's office which took into consideration a fourteen-month term previously imposed on Andretta for another offense. This penalty now was to run concurrently with an indeterminate term of from one to two and a half years in state prison for the Soffer case. In other words, Andretta would be transferred to a state penitentiary after completing his fourteen-month term in a federal prison.

But where was Faugno? No one knew, and at this writing he is still a fugitive from justice.

Investigators say that he vanished from his residence at Edgewood Cliffs in December shortly after the decision admitting the Voiceprint testimony. As far as is known, he has not been seen or heard from since. There are unconfirmed rumors that he may have been a victim of foul play. But the question of his fate remains unanswered. There are many who would like to know.

And another question is still unanswered. Had Andretta been convicted instead of pleading guilty, what would the supreme court have ruled on his appeal? Obviously New Jersey must wait for another trial involving a similar issue to test whether or not Voiceprints will be admitted into the New Jersey courts.

XVII

The Case
of the
Weird Caller

On a quiet Saturday afternoon, February 5, 1966, the calm, relaxing atmosphere of the Red Cross Lounge in the hospital at California's Travis Air Force Base was abruptly changed to one of alarm, fear, and anger. The cause was a telephone call received by the wife of a lieutenant, the last of a series of indecent and threatening messages that had come to two of the hospital's most popular Gray Ladies in the past fortnight.

"I'm going to get you now," was the final threat snarled over the wire in an angry male voice to one of the two victims. Presumably the caller had learned by then that the authorities at the base knew of his actions and had mobilized the Travis police force to bring about his capture as quickly as possible. Revenge obviously accounted for the latest warning.

It was a nerve-wracking situation. In many ways the events that followed were to make history not only in military jurisprudence but in Lawrence Kersta's introduction of Voiceprints as a new weapon against crime. As it was, the case marked the first conviction obtained through the use of his technique, which had never before been tested on a military post. It led not only to a dramatic court-martial but to a lengthy appeal that produced a long written decision regarded by many as one of the most unusual and thorough documents of its kind ever to come from military judges.

Still more, it demonstrated the meticulous, painstaking care taken by the court of air force officers to see justice done; to accord to an enlisted man the same high degree of fairness that would have been expected had the defendant been an officer of high rank.

The affair had its beginning on Saturday, January 22, when two of the women serving as Red Cross hostesses for hospital patients received at their homes on the base anonymous telephone calls from a man using obscene language and concluding with dire threats. In no way did he explain why his two victims had been singled out from among the large number of Gray Ladies, nor did he disclose the motivation for his menacing words. In each case the women made no reply and quickly hung up their telephones. Neither knew of the other's experience until some time later. Each assumed then that she had been called at random by a soldier the worse for drink.

However, on the following day, the lieutenant's wife, Mrs. McIver, was called again and listened to the same indecent and threatening talk that she had heard the day before. More frightened this time than before, she notified Lieutenant Robert C. Marcan, chief of law enforcement on the base.

Realizing at once the critical nature of the situation, Marcan summoned a corps of his men to discuss a plan of action. They were aware that they might be matching wits with a madman with hallucinations who perhaps would not stop at violence; that the safety of many women on the base was in danger. Yet where to start and what measures to take became puzzling questions, since Travis, one of the largest air force bases in the country, located in the city of Fairfield, covers 6,170 acres of sprawling, flat ground, and is often referred to by officers as "a city within a city." At the time more than 10,000 men, women, and children were living within its boundaries.

The first move, they agreed, was to post guards around the homes of the women who had received calls and to strengthen security about their immediate neighborhoods. More than that, they would be alert to any man acting suspiciously and would inquire at the hospital whether there had been unpleasant encounters between Gray Ladies and servicemen; whether anyone in uniform had been overheard making unusual complaints or engaging in violent or indecent talk.

As these measures were being taken, word of the situation became known in some areas of the base, despite all efforts to maintain secrecy. An air of fear spread fast, especially among the women. Some locked their windows and barred their doors; others chose to remain at home rather than risk an outdoor encounter. It was an atmosphere new to the large and friendly air force community.

Here and there frightened women pointed suspiciously at a serviceman said to have been "acting strangely." Such men were watched and in a few cases questioned, but without result.

Meanwhile a trap had been set. Because it was assumed that the mysterious caller had spoken from the telephone booth in the Red Cross Lounge, and probably would do it again, it had been decided to connect the instrument to a concealed tape recorder. At least this might provide the first substantial clue to the wanted man.

Two days of impatient waiting had passed when Mrs. McIver received still another call, and this time she lingered on the line hoping in this way to provide as lengthy a voice recording as possible. At its conclusion she notified Lieutenant Marcan and he hastened to the phone booth. It was empty, and as he looked about he saw a second-class air force private walking alone out of the lounge. Marcan recognized him as James G. Wright, a hospital patient, who had been painfully injured in an automobile accident a few days before. He was known as a quiet, well-mannered person, aged about twenty-seven, and a painter of exceptional talent. In no way did his presence arouse suspicion.

On the following morning Wright was in the Red Cross Lounge talking to a Gray Lady who was interested in having him paint a portrait of her child. The soldier declined because of his injury, but the talk that followed was overheard by Mrs. McIver, who thought she recognized the voice. She walked over to the couple, apologized for the intrusion, and inquired whether

Wright would consider making a canvas of her son. Again he refused. To the lieutenant's wife the artist's voice "sounded like" that of her mysterious caller. Far from certain, however, she reported the incident to Marcan, explaining that she was loathe to involve the young man in trouble because of what, on her part, was little more than a suspicion.

After she had returned home for lunch her telephone rang and once more she listened to the voice that she had heard on the previous days, only this time the speaker was more pugnacious and in angry tones he upbraided her for notifying the authorities, ending with the threat to "get her now."

As soon as Marcan learned of this he sent for Staff Sergeant Gaskell Sauls and together they hastened to the telephone booth in the hospital lounge, surmising that this latest call had come from there. If they had guessed correctly, the message would have been recorded, so they quickly took the tape to headquarters and ran it off. It contained the words that Mrs. McIver had heard. Now, at least, they had their first clue.

On the way back to the hospital they planned a ruse. One of them would engage Wright in conversation to ascertain if by ear they could detect any similarity between his voice and that which they already had heard on tape.

They soon observed Wright sitting relaxed in a lounge chair, his face buried in a magazine. Casually Sauls stepped to his side with a simple question. "Have you got change for a quarter?" he inquired. "I need a dime for the coffee machine."

Wright jumped to his feet and saluted. "Sorry, sir," he said politely, "but I can tell you where to get it."

The two officers exchanged knowing glances, both convinced that they recognized the voice.

Now Sauls, losing no time, came directly to the point. He bluntly informed the young private of his suspicions but suggested that, in fairness, Wright, in his hearing, should telephone to Mrs. McIver, repeating the exact words and phrases that would be given to him. Perhaps, the officer explained, the apparent similarity in voices was only a coincidence.

Wright laughed as if the test would be a lark. "Of course I

won't mind," he said without hesitation. "You know I'd never do a thing like that, especially to a lady."

The test call was soon arranged, and while the two officers listened attentively, Wright spoke as directed.

"You may go now," he was told, the others refraining from any comment, but as he walked away Marcan and Sauls whispered to each other that now they were even more certain that they had found the guilty man.

Before long Wright was summoned to headquarters and told in cold, precise words that he was definitely a suspect. He was informed of his legal rights, advised that he was entitled to counsel, and asked if he was willing to be questioned.

"I know my legal rights," he countered, "and I don't want counsel. Go ahead and question me; I can prove that I had nothing to do with it."

After considerable questioning, during which he repeatedly asserted his innocence, Wright was asked if he would again speak over the telephone to his alleged victim. He had no objections and, after his first conversation, he was directed to repeat the words, speaking this time more slowly and in harsher tones, a procedure that left the officers thoroughly satisfied that they were making no mistake. Mrs. McIver said that the voice "sounded like" the one she had heard but, again in fairness, she could not be as positive as the others.

Soon afterward Wright was placed under arrest and charged with violating the Code of Military Justice Article 134 10USC, a section imposing severe penalties for indecent and threatening telephone calls to women.

Preparations for a court-martial were begun, but in the meantime base officers, who had heard something of Voiceprints, decided to call on Lawrence Kersta for scientific judgment. At his request they sent him their tape recordings of the anonymous calls with tapes of Wright's known voice, requesting a report as quickly as adequate tests could be completed.

A week later the reply came. Kersta's judgment was that beyond doubt the voices were identical. He added that he would be willing to testify as to his findings if this were desired.

The task of assembling a court by now had been completed.

It comprised eleven officers: two colonels, three lieutenant-colonels, three majors, two captains and a lieutenant.

The trial opened in a somber, dramatic setting, the court members resplendent in gold braid and polished buttons. After the formal charges had been read and the accused had entered his plea of not guilty, Mrs. McIver was called to relate the several occurrences. She concluded by stating that now she was "reasonably certain" that the caller's voice was identical to that which she later had heard from the accused.

She was followed by Lieutenant Marcan and his associates, each detailing his role in the events that had led to the arrest.

Over the vigorous objections of the defense, the prosecutor then produced a play-back machine, announcing that he wished the court to hear recordings on the two tapes so that its members could judge for themselves the voice similarity. It was a dramatic moment as the trial officers leaned forward in their chairs, cupping their ears to catch every word and sound.

After a few other witnesses had been heard, Lawrence Kersta was called. He walked briskly to the stand, prepared to meet not only intensive cross-examination at the hands of opposing counsel but to encounter a bitter challenge of Voiceprint values from at least one scientist who he presumed would be called by the defense. He was not disappointed. He had faced this experience before.

Responding to prolonged interrogation by the prosecution, Kersta first listed his qualifications and his professional standing, after which he launched into the basic techniques involved in Voiceprinting.

From this he moved into a narration of his part in the case on trial, telling in minute detail how he had reached his conclusion that the defendant was guilty.

In cross-examination he was peppered for hours with questions intended to trap him in contradictions and to discredit the accuracy of this technique. However, he stood his ground firmly. In no way could he be shaken.

The defense, nevertheless, was far from finished with Kersta. It called to the stand Dr. Frank B. Clark, who identified himself as a research psychologist at Stanford Research Institute in California, specializing in speech transmission. He was by no means complimentary in his appraisal of Kersta's Voiceprints and the methods involved.

Voiceprint identification, he testified, was "far from what we'd term highly realistic," and he implied that the entire process was only emerging from the experimental stage. For more than an hour he elaborated on his views, responding to a multitude of defense questions.

At last, when testimony was finally ended, the court listened to closing arguments. Much time was consumed by defense counsel, who not only insisted that Wright was the victim of mistaken identity but renewed an attack on Voiceprints. Wright's lawyers argued that the scientific principles underlying Voiceprint identification are so uncertain as to require exclusion of this evidence as a point of law. Rules excluding lie detector and truth-serum tests were cited.

The court then retired to deliberate. Wright, still confident of vindication, waited anxiously for the verdict.

Some time later his face fell as he heard the word "guilty."

Rising quickly to his feet, he listened with ashen face as he was sentenced to confinement at hard labor for six months, a bad conduct discharge, and "accessory penalties."

Defense counsel immediately gave notice of appeal, claiming a number of indiscretions in both the investigation and the trial, all of them highly prejudicial to the defendant.

In keeping with military practice, a board of review was created, with Lieutenant Colonel Milton E. Kosa and Colonel Joseph Buchta assigned to direct the appellant's case. Opposing them would be Colonels James R. Thorn and Emanuel Lewis with Lieutenant Colonel David B. Stevens.

Weeks passed before a decision was rendered affirming the judgment of the court-martial. It was a remarkably interesting document, minutely detailed, with only Judge Ferguson dissenting on the ground that in his opinion the value of Voiceprint identification had not been adequately proven. He recommended a rehearing.

The majority of the board of review, however, had spared no words not only in supporting Kersta's tests but in accepting testimony as to the manner in which the tapes of Wright's voice had been obtained, a procedure strongly protested by the defense. In fact, the members of the appeal body, before passing judgment, had listened to the recorded voices themselves.

Because the written decision reflects so interestingly the painstaking efforts of the judges to analyze every element involved in the appeal and to interpret them in accordance with military law, paragraphs of the decision deserve mention here.

Responding to the appellant's claim that he had suffered unjustly because of the recording machine secreted in the telephone booth, the review board stated:

"Secret use of a recording device by one party in a conversation with another in order to make an accurate record of the conversation does not make the testimony as to the content of the conversation inadmissible. The content and circumstances of the conversation determine its admissibility, not the fact that a device is secretly used to make a permanent record of it. Consequently where an accused under investigation for making obscene telephone calls agreed to talk with one of the victims over the telephone for purposes of voice identification, the undisclosed recording of the conversation did not deny or abridge any substantial right of the accused."

Kersta's right to testify as an expert also had been challenged. This, too, was brushed aside by the appeal body, which found that in permitting the developer of Voiceprints to testify "there was no error in admitting this testimony, Kersta having established his qualification as an electronics expert and inventor of the system."

Attention was given to the appellant's contention that the principles of Voiceprinting "are so uncertain in theory and practice that they should be excluded as evidence." This the appeal board also negated, pointing to Kersta's account of his thirty-nine years experience in Bell Laboratories and his detailed accounts of exhaustive and satisfying experiments with his technique. The board wrote:

"Courts have consistently recognized the admissibility of testimony of experts in areas where there is neither infallibility of result nor unanimity of opinion as to the existence of a particular condition or fact. For example, the difference of opinion among psychiatrists as to the mental condition of a person is very well known . . . identifying the author of a questioned document by comparison of the handwriting of a document with other handwritings made by known persons is commonplace in the courts but it certainly cannot be said that all experts in the field are infallible and all techniques of identification are infallible."

The decision continued: "Here the tape recording of one of the obscene calls and the recording of the test call made by the accused were both before the court-martial. Each was played in open court. Since voice identification by ear is usually acceptable in the courts, the court members could thus determine for themselves the margin of error, if any, in Mr. Kersta's opinion. With the board of review, therefore, I am satisfied that the shortcomings of Mr. Kersta's Voiceprint system did not render his opinion inadmissible."

The decision marked another victory for Kersta. As to Wright, it gave him ample time to ponder the irony of his fate. Only three days after the time of his arrest he would have received an honorable medical discharge from the service.

XVIII

Telephones, Terror, and Mothers

Lawrence Kersta sometimes says that Voiceprint identification can save taxpayers' money by inducing people who have committed crimes to plead guilty, thus avoiding the expense of prolonged jury trials.

A case in point, with an unexpected climax, began in the fall of 1970 in the city of Fremont, a busy industrial community of 120,000 southeast of San Francisco Bay. It involved an alarming series of indecent telephone calls to more than ten of the twenty-five young mothers participating in a cooperative child care center where each of them served one day a week looking after the children.

One of the most puzzling elements of the mystery was that all of the women, as a precaution against just what took place, had insisted on having their telephone numbers unlisted. They were known only to the mothers and fathers belonging to the private group, the numbers being provided on typed sheets held only by the parents to facilitate communication in case of necessary changes in the working schedule.

The anonymous calls, all of a sexual nature, began late in October, 1970. At first little attention was paid to them by the busy housewives, but when they continued, growing more offensive and sometimes with implied threats, the mothers began to contact each other and compare their experiences. At last they agreed that a small committee should call on Chief of Police John Fabbri and present the facts.

After listening to what they had to say, the chief sent for Sergeant Gary K. Tyler, then head of a special detail assigned to suppress violence, for Fabbri had concluded that such telephone calls might eventually lead to physical harm.

Tyler, a resourceful officer with eight years of experience on the force, was quick to venture an opinion. "Looks to me like this might be what we call an inside job," he said. "If the phone numbers are unlisted and known only to your group, how could an outsider get them?"

Several women resented the suggestion, insisting that none of their husbands would be guilty of such conduct. One or two suspected that in some way a copy of the numbers had gotten into outside hands. At all events Tyler promised to do all that he could.

Despite his initial efforts, however, the calls not only continued but became bolder and far more offensive, the unidentified speaker finally telling several women that he was determined to have them satisfy his sexual demands.

By now, all of the mothers were terrified, fearing that the tormentor might force his way into a home while the mother was alone and unprotected. Efforts to trace the calls were to no avail and angry husbands began to pressure the police for more effective action.

As weeks slipped by with no diminishing of the trouble, Tyler, in his own mind and with no tangible evidence, had focused suspicious attention on two men. One, he was told, was of "the type" that might find vicarious satisfaction in frightening women; the other was the only father who visited the center. He was a pleasant man about forty years of age, a former athlete, muscularly built. Though he always explained that he had come to the center to assist the women, he never was known to turn a hand, being apparently only interested in unwanted conversation.

Tyler had determined to keep close watch on these two men and to learn what he could of their backgrounds. He was unprepared for a more serious and alarming turn that came in December, only a few days before Christmas.

The terrified victim was an extremely small and attractive woman, Mrs. Philomine Yin, shy and reserved. With her husband, a forty-year-old civil engineer and their two children, she had come to Fremont from mainland China less than two years before. She had been busily at work when the ringing of the telephone interrupted her. She was expecting to hear from her husband but instead she listened to a strange male voice and she became hysterical at what he said.

"I want to come over and hug your pretty little body," he had exclaimed. "Maybe I'll come over right now and we can go to bed together."

Mrs. Yin, badly frightened, hung up her receiver quickly and bolted the front door. An hour later her husband appeared for dinner and asked her what was disturbing her. Hearing her explanation, Yin became extremely upset. As the police learned later he had come from a region in China where husbands regarded such incidents as possible evidence that their wives had indulged in flirtatious conduct and were trying to shift the blame.

While the young woman tried to convince her husband of her innocence, an idea came to her mind. She had recently bought a tape recorder to assist her children in learning English. Now, she thought, why not attach it to her telephone receiver. If the annoyer called again, and she was certain that he would, his words would be preserved and her husband then would know that she had not deceived him.

The second call came two days later, and Yin, listening to the tape on his return home, was entirely appeased. Angry at the mysterious caller, he summoned the police and Sergeant Tyler drove up to the neat one-story stucco home of the Yins. He listened to the offensive words and explained that everything possible was being done. The recording instrument, he said, should be left in place.

Yin was home alone on an afternoon three days later when he answered the telephone and heard a man's voice saying "Hello."

"Who are you and what do you want?" Yin demanded, suspecting from whom the call was coming. The stranger evidently realized his mistake in timing. "Is this Al's Wrecking Works?" he inquired quickly.

Yin shouted an angry "no" and hung up his receiver, thoroughly convinced that the caller had expected Mrs. Yin to answer and had been surprised to hear a male voice.

With this call recorded on tape, Yin related the occurrence to his wife on her return from shopping. "Oh, it's that same man again," she exclaimed excitedly. "I'm sure he thought I was home alone and would answer the phone." Yin agreed.

By now one of the suspects had been eliminated; there remained only the lone male visitor to the child care center. This man, now summoned to headquarters, was Jack D. Coffey, over six feet tall and heavy, known to neighbors for the kindly, gentle way in which he played with his wife's three small children by a previous marriage. His wife, a small woman, accompanied him to Tyler's office and lost no time in berating the sergeant for his suspicions. Speaking for himself, Coffey flatly denied any knowledge of the calls, admitting that he had heard talk of them and could not understand "how anyone could stoop so low." His wife not only echoed his words but bitterly accused Tyler of trying to "frame" an innocent man. She offered no reason for this accusation.

At last Coffey was asked to record his voice on police tape, repeating the exact words and phrases that had been heard by Mrs. Yin. With obvious reluctance he finally agreed to do as he was told, but as he did Tyler and an aide detected apparent nervousness. At times Coffey stumbled over simple words; others he seemed only to mumble.

When the test was over Tyler told the Coffeys that they were no longer needed. "If your husband is as innocent as you say he is," he told the angry wife, "we'll know it in a few days."

The recordings were airmailed at once to Lieutenant Nash for comparison, and Tyler waited anxiously for an answer. It came a few days later in a telephone call from Nash stating that he was reasonably certain of his conclusions but he wanted to hear one more tape of Coffey's voice speaking the words "Al's Wrecking Works." Nash's spectograms of the phrase were not as clear as he would wish before making a final decision.

Reluctantly, Coffey gave the police another recording and it was rushed to the Michigan specialist. This now convinced Nash that beyond doubt that Coffey was the guilty man.

It was time now for the law to act. Coffey was sent for again and advised of his legal rights. He surrendered on a warrant charging a violation of Section 653 M of the Penal Code, which makes obscene telephone calls a misdemeanor. He engaged Attorney Ray Hamrick to defend him, and on his first court appearance pleaded not guilty. It was a simple, perfunctory procedure, in no way foretelling the legal tangle that was to follow.

Assistant District Attorney Michael P. Semansky of Alameda County, assigned to prosecute the case, announced to the court that he was preparing to bring Nash from Michigan as the expert witness for the state, a decision that a few newsmen questioned. "Why go to such expense in a case where no one has suffered violence?" they inquired.

But Semansky, a lawyer brilliant beyond his youthful years, was not to be thwarted in his purpose. If Coffey was guilty, he should be punished, the lawyer explained; the victim, if not physically hurt, had suffered mental anguish. However, he had still another purpose, which he did not reveal at the time. He was convinced that Voiceprints were an effective means of scientific identification and he knew of Nash's reputation. Sometime before, in the Watts arson case, Voiceprint testimony had been declared inadmissible by the state's appellate court; the Hodo appeal decision reversing that earlier judgment had not yet been rendered. Under these circumstances Semansky was hopeful that with progressive advances in the technique, a new legal test, based on the Coffey case, might add California to the list of states accepting Voiceprints as legal evidence. However, he did not know then that his plans would be changed by what unexpectedly occurred sometime later.

In a pretrial session before Municipal Judge Joseph Weber, a visiting jurist from Mendocino County in Northern California, the defense moved to suppress all Voiceprint testimony, contending that the method was not yet adequately developed. Semansky, sensing that Coffey and his lawyer feared the impact of

Voiceprint evidence, challenged the defense motion, citing favorable rulings in other states. Arguments continued for hours until Judge Weber finally spoke the words for which the prosecutor had been hoping. He ruled decisively that he would permit the introduction of Voiceprints, asserting that in his judgment "spectography has advanced sufficiently" to permit its use as evidence. The prosecutor had won his first skirmish, but the legal fight was far from over.

The defense, refusing to accept the court's ruling, entered a new motion, now on technical grounds, to suppress the disputed evidence. Again Coffey lost.

The actual trial opened several months later with Nash prepared to testify as the state's star witness. In the courtroom were professors from Stanford and other universities in the area, anxious to hear what he would say.

Nash, speaking slowly and carefully avoiding technical terms, described his work, telling how he had reached his conclusions. He took pains to emphasize his belief that Voiceprints are as accurate as fingerprints.

"What is the margin of error?" Semansky asked the witness.

"Certainly not over five percent," Nash responded.

"And you feel convinced beyond a doubt that the spectograms made from the recorded voice of the defendant are identical to those made by the recordings of the anonymous calls attributed to him?"

"Beyond a doubt."

To this opinion Nash held steadfastly throughout a barrage of cross-examination.

Coffey's lawyer opened his case by calling to the stand Michael Hecker of Stanford University, who had worked with Voiceprints and was ready to challenge Nash's testimony. He made no effort to belittle the Michigan expert but he insisted that the latter's statement regarding a 5 percent margin of error was too low. In this respect he was supported by Dr. Peter Ladefoged of Southern California.

For a full day defense experts faced the prosecutor's vigorous cross-examination. At day's end Coffey's lawyer moved for a continuance, arguing that the arrest warrant was faulty; that Mrs. Yin had erred in fixing the exact time of one of the offensive calls.

After a date for resumption of the hearing had been set, Coffey's lawyer announced his withdrawal from the case for personal reasons and the court found itself in a quandry. Coffey wanted to serve as his own attorney but the judge demurred, pointing out that the defendant was unprepared to assume that responsibility. He first suggested that a public defender be called but this later proved impossible since Coffey's assets exceeded the maximum set for public defender services. At this point a friend of the accused volunteered his services.

May 15, 1973, had been set for resumption of the trial, the court calendar being unusually heavy at an earlier time. What followed was wholly unexpected.

Long before the date set by the court, Coffey called on the prosecutor and said that he was prepared now to change his plea to one of guilty and beg the court for leniency. Though he did not explain the reasons for his change of mind, it was apparent to all others concerned that he realized by this time that Voiceprints had decided the case against him. It was finally agreed that the charge would be changed to one of a slightly lower degree and Coffey "threw in the sponge."

Before the week was out he appeared before Judge Joseph F. Perly, who had returned to his department to replace the visiting magistrate.

Coffey, with a sheepish, pale look, faced the court as the amended complaint was read. "You have heard the charge," Judge Perly told him. "What do you plead—guilty or not guilty?"

The accused man wet his lips and stared at the jurist, wondering what his fate would be.

"I plead guilty," he said in a voice so low that it was audible only to court attendants.

"Are you ready for sentence?" he was asked.

Coffey nodded.

Judge Perly lectured him severely, emphasizing the seriousness of the offense. Then, acknowledging the fact that the accused had agreed to undergo psychiatric treatment, the judge said that he would be spared a prison term. He was then sentenced to serve a full year on probation.

The mothers in the cooperative nursery were never again troubled by annoying phone calls.

XIX

The Case
of the
"Soul Brother"

For close to two years nuns in forty-five different convents in Detroit and surrounding Michigan cities were subjected to the indignities of a mysterious telephone caller who boldly defied every effort of the police and private detectives to trap him.

That he was finally brought to justice was an achievement for Voiceprints and for Lieutenant Nash, who describes "the case of the 'soul brother'" as one of the strangest, most perplexing in his entire career.

Complicating the long manhunt, and confusing the authorities, was a peculiar, contradictory element. While the caller repeatedly identified himself as black and his victims agreed that he "talked like a southern Negro," every clue pointed to a white man as the culprit.

In every instance he confined his calls to convents and always insisted on talking to a Sister. The voice was invariably the same and there appeared to be little if any deviation in what he said.

While the names of the offended nuns have been withheld by the authorities for obvious reasons, they have disclosed that the institutions selected for outrageously indecent calls included the Sisters of St. Francis Convent in Detroit, St. Athanasius Convent in Roseville, and the Sisters of Charity Convent in Lansing. There were many others in various parts of the state.

In every call, without exception, the speaker began by announcing that "this is your soul brother," and he always made certain that a nun was on the other end of the telephone. He would then hesitate for a few moments before launching into a tirade of vulgar, obscene, and suggestive language. Time and again his victims told him bluntly that they had nothing to say and were ready to hang up their receivers. His response was always the same:

"I know why you won't talk to me; it's because I'm black."

The first call, received at a Detroit convent in an afternoon early in 1971, in no way suggested that this would be the beginning of what actually became a reign of terror. The nun receiving the abusive message hastened to tell her Mother Superior what had occurred and they decided to notify the police.

The telephone company was contacted but, of course, it was too late to trace the call. A tape recorder was attached to the telephone in the event of a repeated message, but the authorities were inclined to view this as an isolated offense, probably the work of a mentally disturbed person acting on impulse.

Their surmise proved incorrect, for a few days later a similar complaint came from another convent in the same city and afterward from other communities in scattered parts of Michigan.

Before long the offense was continued on a still more daring and persistent scale. In one case, close to forty calls were made to the same convent in less than three hours.

Telephone company technicians spent days trying to trace the calls, but this was found to be impossible because all the calls had come from an older part of Detroit where a peculiar type of equipment was in use.

Nevertheless a number of voice recordings on magnetic tape had been obtained at various convents, and although the police still were without a single tangible clue that might lead to a suspect, they decided to consult Lieutenant Nash, for it already had been agreed that this was definitely a case requiring the use of Voiceprints.

Though Nash at this point would be seriously handicapped without a sample of a suspect's known voice, the authorities believed that he might at least suggest some new and more effective course of investigation.

The Michigan expert went to work, though he was only able to subject the tapes to aural evaluation. Before long he had reached a definite conclusion.

"The caller in these cases," he reported, "in my opinion is a white man deliberately disguising his voice to make it appear that he is black."

In Detroit investigators read the opinion, shook their heads and smiled. They had been convinced from the start that they should be looking for a black man and they had ample reason for their judgment. Not only had the foul-mouthed speaker taken pains to assert his color, a statement verified by all who had heard him, but there was still further evidence to support their theory.

A black woman, holding an important position in the telephone company, already had listened to the tapes and declared that she was certain beyond doubt that the inflection was that of a southern Negro.

Another puzzling factor in the hunt was the fact that the elusive caller confined himself to convents. Exhaustive inquiries had been made to ascertain whether anyone outside of the church had been annoyed. None could be found. This, of course, led to the belief that the man was a fanatic with religious prejudices, perhaps retaliating for a wrong he believed had been done by someone in the church.

Months of fruitless police work had passed before what appeared to be the first worthwhile clue came to light. A telephone company technician, resorting to what is known as "manual tracing," had learned the number from which he felt confident that at least one of the calls had come.

But this subscriber was white, and inquiry revealed that he had an untarnished record, having been employed in an important post by a large corporation. He had two sons who lived at home with their parents. The youngest was a twenty-four-year-old veteran returned from Vietnam; the other held a responsible government position in Detroit.

Detectives, weighing these facts, reasoned that an error probably had been made, yet the telephone investigators were equally positive of the accuracy of their report.

"If you are so certain," one of the detectives argued, "how can you account for the conflict in facts—a white family, responsible people, and a Vietnam veteran for a son?"

The telephone men were at a loss for answer. Though fully recognizing the discrepancies, they remained firm in their belief that they had made no mistake. "It could well be," one of them theorized, "that someone has made an illegal connection with the line that we've identified and hooked up with another phone—a rare piece of skulduggery to be sure, but it's been done. That would account for what's confusing us."

How to proceed in the face of such a possibility posed a perplexing problem. Too much time already had been lost and complaints of continuing calls to convents were still being received week after week.

Telephone workmen checked the cables diligently, inch by inch, looking for evidence of a hooked-in line, but nothing of the sort could be found. They were finally obliged to admit that their surmise was worthless.

On a mere hunch, Police Sergeant Richard Scott, who had been one of the most active among the investigators, decided on a move of his own. He called the number that had been reported by the telephone workers and asked to speak to Robert Piku, the youngest son of the family. With Voiceprint possibilities uppermost in his mind, he had carefully adjusted a tape recorder to his telephone.

Scott proceeded cautiously, careful not to even intimate an accusation or a suspicion. He told Robert Piku the nature of his investigation, suggesting that perhaps the young veteran might have a clue.

To his surprise Piku took the inquiry in bad form. In fact, he became highly indignant and flatly refused to continue the conversation.

Despite Scott's frustration, his call had been to good purpose. At least he had a taped record of the man's voice, the first vital clue in the long investigation. The sergeant, of course, was by no means certain that his lead would be of value; the answer, spelling success or failure, would come from Voiceprints.

The recording of Piku's voice was sent at once to Lieutenant Nash, along with more tapes made at the various convents that had received abusive calls.

In East Lansing, Nash went to work in his usual way and his report left no doubt but that Scott's suspicions were well founded.

"The voices are identical in every respect," he advised the Detroit police. "By every test your suspect Piku is the man who called the nuns."

Sergeant Scott now was ready for decisive action. Based on the Voiceprint evidence, he obtained a warrant for Robert Piku's arrest and went with it to the latter's home.

Members of the family were astounded, insisting that undoubtedly a serious mistake had been made. But Robert was not at home. He had left several days before on a trip. No one knew where he was or when he would return.

Several months passed during which a close watch was kept for the wanted man. Significantly, the calls to convents had ceased abruptly, another reason that convinced the police that they were moving in the right direction.

Authorities in nearby communities were asked to look for young Piku, but he could not be found. The situation turned into a waiting game.

Suddenly, long after the issuance of the warrant, a convent in a small community more than seventy-five miles from Detroit, received a telephone call from a man who said he was "a soul brother." He used the same salacious language that others had heard before the sudden lapse, and again said that he was black. It was apparent that the fugitive had returned to the area, though he still was not at home.

However, through arrangements that had been made previously between the police and telephone officials, it was possible at this time to trace the call. It had come from what is known as a "boiler room," a large office with many telephones used by trained people to solicit funds for charitable causes.

When Sergeant Scott and two other officers reached the place some time later, they found twelve men busy at their phones. Some of them were black.

Calling the foreman into an adjoining room, Scott inquired whether Robert Piku was known there. "Sure he is," replied the other, pointing to a bright-faced, well-dressed young man seated at a desk. "That's him over there; the third from the left. He's one of our solicitors."

The sergeant, thinking fast, decided to question each member of the crew individually and alone, leaving Piku for the last.

"Have you telephoned to a convent today or in the last several months?" Scott inquired of each man. One after another shook his head, asking curiously what had prompted the question. The officer explained and he soon received significant information that he had not expected.

"I did hear this man Piku using obscene language over his phone today," one of the solicitors volunteered. "But I have no idea who he was speaking to."

The suspect, six feet tall and heavily built, was called from his work. He was informed that he was under arrest and told briefly the reason why.

Piku's face paled. He wet his lips and stood silently staring at the officers.

"You might as well admit it," one of the policemen said. "You were overheard today using obnoxious language over your phone."

For moments the young man looked at those about him—and then he nodded.

"Yes, I did call a convent this morning like you say," he blurted. "I guess I must be crazy."

However, he vigorously denied having made any of the other calls, and even after days of questioning he remained adamant on this point.

He was told to get his hat and coat. Minutes afterward he was on his way to jail. It was now late in the winter of 1972, almost two years since the first convent call had been made.

On the following day he appeared for arraignment before Judge Mary McDevit of the Thirty-ninth District Court, accompanied by his lawyer. Edward L. Bohde, who previously had authorized issuance of the arrest warrant, appeared for the state.

Though defense counsel knew of the Voiceprint findings, Piku pleaded not guilty, indicating that he was prepared to fight for acquittal. Hours later he was released on bond, his trial having been set for a day several weeks later.

Evidently Piku had seriously considered the strength of the case against him, for when he appeared in court again, he unexpectedly entered a plea of guilty.

Judge McDevit, no doubt aware that the defendant was badly in need of medical help, sentenced him to six months' imprisonment and immediately granted probation on condition that he remain out of trouble and obtain psychiatric treatment at once.

The calls to nuns had already ceased. Their motivation probably is a well-guarded secret in the files of a psychiatrist.

XX

A Dubious Distinction

Armistice Day—November 11, 1970—brought no sense of peace to comely Mrs. Betty Phoenix of Indianapolis, the short, slightly built mother of seven children—two girls and five sons.

To the contrary, the day's events enmeshed her in a series of strange and curious conflicts that were to give her the dubious distinction of being probably the second woman in America ever found guilty through the use of Voiceprint evidence.

However, time and intensive police activity would precede her arrest for making three menacing bomb threats over the telephone.

Despite the holiday, Betty Phoenix had reported for work as usual at the North Shadeland plant of the Western Electric Company, contributing her expertise at a punch press to her employer's manufacture of telephones. It was a job that she had held for a considerable time and wanted to keep, for she was separated from her husband and permanent employment was essential.

The first unusual occurrence on this Armistice Day came a few minutes after 9:30 in the morning when Mae Johnson, a secretary in Western Electric's labor relations office, answered her telephone and listened to a woman's voice with a bitter complaint about her treatment as an employee. Speaking angrily, the caller demanded to know why she had been laid off a few weeks previously for several days when others were compelled to work overtime. She further said that her husband, having recently returned from Vietnam, could not find work and funds were needed to support the couple and their children.

Miss Johnson's immediate response was that she was unable to provide an answer without investigation. As the secretary reported to her superiors a short time later, "the woman told me that pretty soon we wouldn't have anything to worry about because the whole place would be blown to bits. With that she hung up the phone with a bang."

"Was there anything distinctive about the voice?" Miss Johnson was asked.

Though she replied negatively, she did express an opinion that the call had come from inside the plant.

"What gives you that idea?" the department manager inquired.

"I could tell, I think, by the ringing of the bell," Miss Johnson explained. "Outside calls ring longer, somehow, and this ring was rather short and jerky. When you answer the phone as often as I do, you seem to be able to distinguish calls from the outside, but, of course, I might be wrong."

It was decided that word of the mysterious message, with its warning of a bombing, be kept from the company's many employees, all of whom were busy at their individual tasks. Nevertheless, the police were notified and requested to send only plainclothesmen, since the appearance of officers in uniform would likely cause alarm and perhaps even a degree of panic.

The place was carefully searched without result and Miss Johnson was instructed that in the event of a second call she should try to prolong the conversation, leaving her phone only long enough to call the police. There was a possibility that they could trace the call. She received no further messages of the kind—but others did.

Little more than an hour and a half had passed when a peculiar call reached the Marion County sheriff's office. It was from a woman speaking with obvious agitation. "I am calling," she said, "to let you know there has been a bomb placed in

Western Electric. They have been notified. That will teach them to lay off people and then work overtime."

"Who's speaking—where are you?" the officer demanded, but the speaker had hung up her telephone.

The sheriff's office already had been alerted to what had occurred at the company's headquarters and the deputy at once recognized the similarity of words. He had wanted to continue the conversation in the hope of tracing the call, but the woman may have suspected his purpose.

The mysterious voice, however, was recorded by a tape machine in accord with general practice among law-enforcement agencies in the county. The recording would provide useful Voiceprints should the caller be apprehended.

While the sheriff's men were inclined to attribute the message to a crank or a mentally disturbed person, a detail was posted around the Western Electric building as a precaution after a second and equally thorough search of the place had been made. This had given employees some knowledge of trouble, and excited talk soon was interfering with routine work.

Such was the situation near eleven o'clock that morning when a seventeen-year-old boy, William Vogel, at home because of the school holiday, answered the telephone and heard a woman asking in an excited voice to speak with his father at once.

"He's not here now," the youth responded, but, as he would report soon afterward, his caller continued with a rapid, clipped-voice conversation which at first he found himself unable to follow. Something was said, he related, about "overtime," but the speaker, suddenly talking more slowly, informed him that there was a bomb at Western Electric "set to go off some time today" and he was told to call his mother who customarily worked close to Mrs. Phoenix.

The boy did as he was told and his mother, Mrs. Dorothy Vogel, immediately reported what she had heard to her supervisor. She later confided her fears to her co-worker, Mrs. Phoenix, who already had heard whispered rumors and admitted that "she was uneasy over the bomb threats."

Mystery heightened at 12:30, only three hours after the
first call, when Floyd W. Adkins, a plant supervisor, was called
on the telephone by an unidentified woman advising him that the
plant would be blown up.

As she spoke, suspicion ran through Adkins' mind. He
sensed that he detected an accent that he had previously noted in
Betty Phoenix's speech though it was difficult to describe. Her
voice had a peculiar nasal quality and a trace of a southern drawl.

Adkins hastened to that section of the plant where the
woman worked. She was not at her machine, and on inquiring,
he was told that she was at lunch. It was then that he recalled
having seen her twice at the telephone during the morning but
he had thought nothing of it at the time since management had a
liberal policy in granting workers such privileges.

He was still weighing the possibility of the woman's
involvement in the morning's events when the telephone rang
again. This time his wife was calling to report a peculiar message
she had received only minutes before. "Something has just
happened that I can't understand," Mrs. Adkins said. "Some
woman just phoned me to say that you were having lunch with
another woman. Before I could ask who she was she hung up."

"Did she have a peculiar voice—something like a southern
drawl, or maybe sort of nasal?" Adkins inquired.

"Now that you mention it, she did," the wife said, still
disturbed.

Adkins knew now that his suspicions were well founded and
he lost no time in meeting with top officials of the plant. Though
it seemed incredible that the attractive, industrious Mrs. Phoenix
could have been the caller, there was nothing to do but to advise
the police of their suspicions.

The authorities, fully realizing the seriousness of the
situation, were anxious to proceed cautiously. What they wanted
most was some verification; they were far from ready to confront
Betty Phoenix with a formal accusation.

Their first move was to bring the voice recording made at
the sheriff's office to the Western Electric plant to be played in
the privacy of the labor relations office where Mrs. Johnson,

listening attentively, declared that beyond doubt she was listening to the voice of Mrs. Phoenix.

The officers, however, desired still further proof. They sent for young William Vogel and he was equally positive in his identification. His mother had accompanied him and after hearing the taped voice she, too, said she was certain.

"Just how sure can you be?" detectives inquired. "Remember, a woman's liberty may depend on your answer."

For a few moments Mrs. Vogel hesitated, obviously embarrassed at having to involve a fellow worker. Then, realizing her responsibility, she asserted that she could not be mistaken because she had worked side by side with Mrs. Phoenix for close to three years. Her conclusion, she added, was even further strengthened by the suspect's earlier comment that she was "uneasy about the bomb threats."

There was no reason to delay further action. Betty Phoenix was summoned to police headquarters, and when she appeared detectives found it difficult to believe that this attractive woman with bright blue eyes, well-coiffured brown hair and light complexion could have been responsible for the strange series of bomb scares.

She met all questions with confidence and showed no sign of nervousness. "You're making a terrible mistake," she declared emphatically. "Why should I do such a horrible thing?"

When they told her of the several positive voice identifications she became even more indignant, asserting again that her accusers had erred. In the end, she was told to return home; that there would be still further investigation. The authorities, though now fully convinced of the woman's guilt, were of no mind to move too hastily.

John E. Hirschman, Assistant United States Attorney, was consulted, and after hearing all the facts he formally authorized the arrest and prosecution of Mrs. Phoenix under the newly enacted Title XI, the Organized Crime Act. Specifically she would be accused of violating a federal statute making it a crime to use a telephone "or other instrument of commerce" to make threatening calls.

It was agreed that Voiceprint evidence should be obtained to strengthen and corroborate the testimony of those who already had said that they recognized the woman's voice.

This move was especially approved by Richard L. Brim, investigator for the Treasury Department's Alcohol, Tobacco and Firearms Bureau, who pointed out that this would provide the opportunity for a significant test of the admissibility of Voiceprints in Indiana, where the technique never had been utilized.

It was decided to proceed with Voiceprint comparisons before making an arrest. Mrs. Phoenix was informed that since she persisted in protesting her innocence, such a test could end in vindication, though it might act adversely. The decision was hers to make.

She did not hesitate, agreeing at once to provide a sample of her voice by speaking into a tape recorder that had been brought to her home. The words she uttered were those that had been taped at the sheriff's office.

"You can see that I have nothing to be afraid of," she said, after the sample tape had been obtained.

"Time will tell," was the officer's only comment.

Without delay the recording was sent to Dr. Tosi and Lieutenant Nash in a package that also contained the then unidentified voice. Now it was for them to speak the final words determining the woman's guilt or innocence.

Exactly a week later, after the two men had concluded their study, Nash reported to the government men that their work had proved conclusively that the telephone calls had been made "by Mrs. Phoenix and no one else."

An arrest warrant followed and with it two federal officers proceeded to the Western Electric plant shortly before three o'clock on the afternoon of December 3, 1970. They were escorted to the bench where Betty Phoenix was busily operating her machine. Since numbers of men and women were working close by, the federal men chose to proceed as quietly as possible to avoid undue excitement.

A light tap on the shoulder drew the accused woman's attention from her work and as she stared at the two men standing beside her, they whispered that she was under arrest.

"But I didn't do anything," she pleaded. "I've told that to the officers so many times."

She was shown the warrant, and with tears in her eyes she backed away slowly from her bench and accompanied the men to the jail.

A week later the matter was presented to a federal grand jury and an indictment was returned.

Because of crowded calendars, the case was not called until January 8 of the following year, when Mrs. Phoenix pleaded not guilty. The government was represented by William Andrew Kerr, then an Assistant United States Attorney and now a law professor at Indianapolis Law School at Indiana–Purdue University in Indianapolis. Federal Judge S. Hugh Dillin appointed G. Terry Cutter to conduct the defense.

The three-day trial before a jury began April 14, five months after the bombing phone calls.

First those who had received the calls were asked to relate the circumstances and their identification of the defendant's voice as that of the speaker.

The tape recordings obtained at the sheriff's office then were played for the jury, followed by the sample of Mrs. Phoenix's voice.

Dr. Tosi then took the stand to tell in lay terms the technique of Voiceprinting and to explain why he believed in the reliability of the process.

Defense counsel sharply criticized his confidence in the spectograph. "I might say everybody believes in the machine," Tosi retorted. "There is no person that doesn't."

"You say there is not a person in the United States that doesn't believe in the machine?" snapped Defense Attorney Cutter.

"The machine—no," Tosi was quick to answer, "because the machine is good and never was objected to. Prior to my experiments [at Michigan State University] there was a doubt in the scientific community that the procedure for the spectograms, the product of the machine, could be used very reliably to identify persons."

At present, he emphasized, the process has gained general acceptance.

Lieutenant Nash followed as the second witness, telling exactly how he had made his comparisons and what they revealed. His long and detailed explanation of the incriminating graphs provided the jurors with what really amounted to a word picture of the telephone calls.

"My conclusion," he finally testified, "is that the unknown caller—the voice of the unknown caller—is the same as that of Betty Phoenix."

Under cross-examination, Attorney Cutter tried his best to lead the witness into contradictions. "I am a little amazed," Cutter began. "You said that the voice on the known tape was the same as the one on the government's known tape—that of Betty Phoenix and nobody else, is that true?"

"Yes, that is true," Nash answered, emphasizing his words.

"No one else in the world?" Cutter pressed.

"That is my opinion—yes."

The defense, however, was still not satisfied. "What effect would it have on this particular test, say, if you ran one on myself and I had some teeth taken out and after that you had the same test run?" Cutter inquired. "Would that change anything?"

Nash shook his head before replying, "No, it would not."

"Does any operation on the mouth—would that affect it?" the defense lawyer went on.

Nash's answer brought laughter in the courtroom. "Well," he replied slowly, "if the operation prevented you from speaking—it would, yes."

The attorney followed quickly with still another inquiry. "Maybe I had false teeth put in—all false teeth. That wouldn't affect my voice?"

"No sir, it would not," the expert rejoined. "It would affect your voice but it wouldn't affect this technique."

Questioning now shifted in a new direction. Much time was spent establishing Nash's qualifications.

Betty Phoenix was her own key witness. A pathetic figure, only two inches taller than five feet, she stepped hesitantly to the witness chair to deny her guilt. Her cross-examination was gruelling, but Kerr, the prosecutor, found himself unable to trap her in misstatements.

It took the jury only three hours to find Mrs. Phoenix guilty.

Judge Dillin dismissed the jurors, thanking them for their services and telling them that he, too, would have voted for conviction. He said that he wanted time to consider a proper sentence, and on June 11, 1971 he set her term as one year in prison. Betty Phoenix burst into tears.

Shortly afterward, the judge, presumably considering the woman's responsibilities to her five children, reduced the sentence to fifteen days.

The authorities made no public comment on the penalty, but they were gratified over the first acceptance of Voiceprints in Indiana.

Since the unfortunate woman persisted in denying her guilt, the precise motive for the bomb threats was never fully learned, though she was believed to have reacted to a nervous upset over what she considered to be unfair treatment by her employers.

XXI

Bomb Clues Corroborated

Rom W. Powell, first assistant state attorney, walked out of the Orange County Courthouse in Orlando, Florida, with the air of a satisfied lawyer who had just won a difficult case.

He had every right to be pleased, for the trial marked the first use of Voiceprints as legal evidence in the southern state. Actually, the verdict of guilty had still further significance; it supported a point stressed by many lawyers. Voiceprints, they often say, are of intrinsic value as corroborative testimony. In this case they verified the validity of a tiny fingerprint whose importance the defense had tried its best to belittle.

For these reasons Powell had just told a newsman that "the verdict tonight is a significant event for law enforcement in Florida."

The trial, which started May 3, 1971, had involved two false bomb alarms, the first completely upsetting the calm of Orlando police headquarters, necessitating the evacuation of frightened prisoners and worried officers.

Almost seven months before, on October 17, 1970, the first alarm had reached Policeman William Poole, acting as desk sergeant at the station. Busily scanning the last reports of the night's events, Poole looked up from his work at the ringing of the telephone and noted that it was exactly 6:20 in the morning; the day watch would be reporting soon.

"There's a bomb in the station," said a male voice. "It's

going off at exactly seven ten," and a click at the other end of the line told the officer that the caller had hung up his receiver.

Poole was thinking fast. Dialing for the operator, he asked that every effort be made immediately to trace the menacing call. Moments later he was shouting orders to officers in other parts of the building, directing them to quickly remove a number of prisoners locked in cells and to evacuate the station with the greatest possible speed.

The telephone rang again. Poole reached for the receiver and heard the same voice telling him that a second bomb had been placed in the Orlando Utilities Building. The patrolman tried to stall for time, asking questions in the hope that the call could be traced, but again there was only silence on the line.

Time was passing quickly. Less than twenty minutes remained before the moment set for the bombing. Officers already had started scurrying through the place in a frantic effort to locate an explosive or anything that even resembled a bomb. They could find nothing. The night force at the Utilities Building already had been warned.

Suddenly the phone sounded for a third time. Officer Poole, not far away, hastened to answer, wondering whether he would receive word of still another bomb. Instead the call was from a man in the telephone office with vital information.

"We've traced that call," he announced excitedly, with obvious understanding of the seriousness of the situation.

"From where?" Poole demanded.

"A pay booth in front of a store at 2127 West Washington Street."

Moments later the word went to the radio operator who broadcast an emergency alarm that sent half a dozen patrol cars speeding on their way with orders to converge at the telephone booth.

Meanwhile others had busied themselves with necessary duties. Prisoners were loaded into a van and driven to a parking place some distance away. The police station was now completely empty, its radio man, the last to leave, having set up a portable station in a lot nearby. And for safety of the public, a wide area had been blocked off around the police building.

When the patrol cars arrived at the pay station they found it empty. While one officer quickly dusted the telephone for fingerprints, others scurried about looking for anyone who could be questioned.

It was not necessary for them to look far. Within easy sight they saw a man in his late twenties driving into a gas station in a Chevrolet truck.

"Did you just make a call from that booth over there?" he was asked.

The stranger shook his head. Then, pointing to a Cadillac a short distance away, he suggested that its driver might have used the telephone. The big car was stopped, but its owner satisfied the officers that he was not involved.

They had returned to question the first man when Officer John Brewer interrupted with interesting information. "Say, that's the same guy who was talking to me in the coffee shop an hour or so ago this morning and I'm still wondering what he was getting at."

"Well, what did he say?" one of the patrolmen inquired.

"Just this," Brewer answered. "As well as I can remember he said: 'I'd like to tell you something but if I did you'd arrest me.' I tried to draw him out but he just clammed up.

"Come to think of it now," Brewer went on, "before he left the counter he remarked right out of thin air that a bomb had been placed on the Meyer Motor Inn here three days before the arrival of a very important person, but that it had been removed. I asked him how he knew all this, but he said he'd better shut up; and he left the place."

The man with the truck to whom Brewer referred admitted the conversation, though he tried to laugh it off. He said his name was Joseph Luvon Worley and he still insisted that he had not used the telephone.

Worley, who said he was twenty-seven years of age, was still answering questions when an employee of the nearby store, John Twombly, who had been listening to the conversation, volunteered that he had seen Worley's truck parked in front of the phone booth.

"What about that?" Worley was asked.

He nodded. "Yes, I might as well admit it," he said meekly. "I didn't want to tell you because I was phoning my girl friend and I didn't want my wife to know about it."

"What's the girl's name?" an officer demanded.

Worley's face fell. "Well, it wasn't really a girl," he said, contradicting himself. "It was a man, but the line was busy, so I left."

He had said enough—or too much for his own good. He was told that he was under arrest and informed of his legal rights.

Though Worley still claimed that he knew nothing of the bomb threats, the police were certain that they had the right man. How to prove it with more than circumstantial evidence became their problem.

Experts in the Identification Bureau soon announced that the faint print of a fingertip taken from the underside of the telephone receiver matched with Worley's. Now they had their first bit of direct evidence, but they were convinced that more was needed. They knew of Voiceprints, which never had been used in Florida, and after some consideration it was agreed that this case would provide a good opportunity to test the new method of detection.

The three calls to the police station had been recorded as were all other messages of importance. Now only a sample of Worley's voice was necessary and this was easily obtained by questioning him again at headquarters.

To the investigators the recorded voices appeared to be similar but, of course, expert judgment would be required. The Orlando police already knew of Lieutenant Nash's reputation as an authority in the field, so they sent their tapes and requested his opinion.

As they expected, Nash reported that he had compared spectograms and had found them similar in every detail; that Worley beyond doubt was the bomb-threat caller.

Worley's trial opened May 1, 1971, in Orlando before Criminal Court Judge Warren Edwards, who already had indicated that he would permit the introduction of Voiceprint evidence if a proper basis for its scientific accuracy could be established.

Rom Powell, the assistant state attorney who had been assigned to conduct the prosecution, already was prepared to meet the challenge.

After first leading Officer Poole and his colleagues through detailed recitals of the early stages of the case, Powell cited several decisions in which Voiceprints had been approved as acceptable evidence.

As his next step, he called Dr. Tosi to the stand to explain the technique involved in Voiceprints and the results he had obtained through his intensive studies. Judge and jury listened attentively as Tosi declared that the percentage of error in Voiceprints was "negligible."

Judge Edwards interrupted occasionally to pose a clarifying question, then finally agreed that this type of evidence might be introduced. Florida now had joined the increasing number of states accepting Kersta's methods.

Lieutenant Nash was the next expert witness. In response to Powell's questions he related how he had tested the voice samples and had compared spectograms until he was thoroughly convinced that they were of the same person.

Worley, in his own defense, again denied his guilt and his attorney, in final argument, did his best to deprecate the partial fingerprint, which he insisted was little more than a smudge from which no worthwhile conclusion could be made. Nash's testimony also came in for vigorous attack, the lawyer arguing that the method was new, unreliable, and not worthy of serious consideration. He called attention to decisions in other states supporting this contention.

Now, in rebuttal, Prosecutor Powell hammered hard in pointing out that Voiceprints had served as corroborating evidence. Not one test, but two, he argued, had proved the state's case beyond doubt. Worley's face blanched and the six members of the jury nodded as if in agreement.

The jurors finally retired after listening to the judge's

instructions. They returned to the courtroom only fifteen minutes later with a verdict of guilty.

A few days afterward Worley stood before Judge Edwards and said he was ready to learn his punishment.

Looking down from the bench, the judge reminded Worley of the gravity of his offense. "It is the judgment of this court," he concluded, "that you be confined in state prison for a period of three years."

The convicted man sank back in his seat looking desperately at his lawyer.

A motion for a new trial, challenging the admissibility of Voiceprint evidence, was made and denied. A month later an appeal on the same grounds was filed with the Fourth District Court of Appeal.

More than a year had passed before the high court rendered its decision. Not only did it affirm the verdict of the lower tribunal, approving the introduction of Voiceprint evidence, but it went still further in expressing its support of the technique and its effectiveness.

The importance of the expert testimony by Tosi and Nash was stressed by the appeal judges, whose acceptance of Voiceprints went even beyond that of some jurists in other states.

In his opinion Judge J. Mager offered his own overall views on the need for innovative methods of scientific crime detection such as Voiceprints. He wrote:

"In this day and age when crime rates approach alarming proportions and where recent decisions of the United States Supreme Court establish stringent guidelines in the investigative, custodial and prosecutional areas, a premium is placed upon the development and use of scientific methods of crime detection. Protecting society from those who have violated the law as well as protecting the one who has been unjustly accused serves to heighten the need for more sophisticated methods of crime prevention and crime detection. The use of spectograph voice identification, or 'Voiceprints,' can become an effective tool in identifying the perpetrators of telephone bomb threats, extortions, kidnapers as well as persons making obscene telephone calls.

"Correspondingly, scientific methods of voice identification can serve to virtually eliminate those instances where the wrong person has found himself unjustly charged or under suspicion."

Then turning to the legal aspects of the case, he continued:

". . . what I am suggesting is a recognition that voice identification based upon scientific techniques approaching the character of experimentation reflected in this case, ought to be admissible into evidence as 'direct evidence' in addition to its admissibility as corroborating evidence. . . .

"Doubtless there are those who will question the reliability of voice spectograms and its general scientific acceptance. However, the accuracy of these experiments has reached the degree where its admissibility should be less open to question. . . ."

After citing earlier decisions, he added:

"Again, I should stress that admissibility should not be confused with credibility. The fact that Voiceprint testimony may be admissible does not mean that the jury is categorically bound by such testimony or in any way restrained from being able to determine the proper weight to be given to such testimony. My faith in the jury system leads me to believe that it will be given the weight that the situation and circumstances may dictate. . . ."

A lone dissenting opinion came from Associate Judge Joseph S. White, who indicated that he was not thoroughly convinced of the reliability of Voiceprints because of their newness. Beyond that he called attention to the possibility of error through disguised or mimicked voices.

This was before Kersta's spectograms had betrayed the attempts of widely known professional entertainers to successfully imitate the voices of famous people.

Part 3

STRANGE
CASES IN
HIGH PLACES

XXII

Kersta's
Big Scoop

Not all of Lawrence Kersta's dramatic cases have been concerned with extortion, threats of violence, obscene telephone calls, or other crimes in which the human voice is involved. He perhaps takes greatest pride in one with grave international complications in which charges of foreign intrigue were a major factor.

This occurred on an extremely crucial day when the United States and Great Britain were eagerly attempting to unravel a strange and unusual mystery. Peace in the Middle East was an all-important element.

Yet the possibility of becoming a key figure in an enigma of such complex proportions was furthest from Kersta's mind that June morning in 1968 when he received a telephone call from the New York office of the *London Daily Telegraph* virtually begging for his professional services.

It was a day when he faced an unusually strenuous schedule calling for morning conferences in his office and two speaking engagements in the afternoon. But the importance of the startling request gave it top priority.

Kersta's morning had followed the customary routine: breakfast with his wife, casual talk about her plans for the day, and a hurried reading of a New York newspaper. As usual he scanned the pages, giving major attention to such world affairs as interested him most and to happenings in scientific fields.

He read of serious new tensions in the Middle East with fears of a resumption of the Six Day War of 1967. However, he had pressing local affairs on his mind and the Middle East was far away.

The wholly unexpected telephone message that abruptly changed his schedule came soon after he had reached his office and started to open his mail.

"A most serious and perplexing situation has arisen," said his caller, after explaining that both the London newspaper and the CBS television network were eager for his help, hoping to score what might be a tremendous news beat.

"The United States and Great Britain are both seriously concerned," the speaker continued. "Could your Voiceprints establish the authenticity of a very popular kind of telephone conversation?"

"It all depends on circumstances and what's involved," Kersta replied, making it clear that before venturing an answer he would need to know exactly what had occurred. He does not recall the exact words of the response he received but in substance he was informed that only a few hours before a press conference in Jerusalem had brought to light what either was a brazen case of international intrigue or a hoax. The *Daily Telegraph* and CBS-TV needed almost immediately to know which was the case.

Pressing hard for further details, Kersta was told that the press conference in Israel had been called by Colonel Moshe Perlman, a pioneer leader in his country's public relations program, who had read to correspondents from several nations the transcription of a tape recording of what the Israelis insisted had been a telephone conversation between the president of the United Arab Republic, Gamal Abdel Nasser, and King Hussein of Jordan—a daring verbal exchange in which the speakers were plotting to publicly blame the United States and Britain for the Arab defeat in the previous year's fighting.

The purported exchange between the two top Arabs had been in Arabic but was easily understood by astute intelligence officers of the Israeli army. Allegedly it had taken place two days before, the exact day that the Arab countries had severed diplomatic relations with America and Britain, accusing them of giving heavy military air support to Israel. How the Israelis had succeeded in listening in on the purported message was not explained, but their spokesman assured his press audience that the words of the Arabs had been recorded on tape.

As Kersta listened to these facts, given to him by telephone from a New York spokesman for the London paper, he sensed the excitement of his caller and doubtful thoughts were running through his mind. Still not knowing exactly how Voiceprints could be utilized in such a situation, he was wondering whether he was prepared to tackle such a problem; moreover he was weighing the delicate diplomatic factors that might be involved if he undertook an assignment such as this. However, he was facing one of the most challenging tasks he had ever been asked to perform and the thought of playing an important role in such a drama thoroughly intrigued him. He decided to play for time by again insisting on further details.

"Excuse my interruption," he told his caller. "This is certainly exciting, but do the tapes tell exactly what the Israelis claim was said?"

"That they most certainly do," the other replied. "The tapes as read in Israel at the press meeting were reread to us here by our Jerusalem representative as well as to our London office and recorded at both places. Just listen carefully now and I'll read them to you as we've taken them off of the relayed tape."

Kersta pressed the receiver still closer to his ear and this is what he heard:

Hussein: "The United States and England."

Nasser: "My God, I say that I will make an announcement and you will make an announcement and we will see to it that the Syrians make an announcement that American and British airplanes are taking part against us from aircraft carriers. . . ."

The recorded conversation, according to the Israelis, had ended with a few pleasantries.

Kersta could barely believe his ears. "Did the Israel colonel disclose how such an amazing thing ever got into Israel's hands?" he inquired.

"Certainly not, but smart army people have ways, you

know. What we must know—and know fast—is whether that recording is genuine, or was it, shall we say, deliberately faked."

"What's the reaction in the Middle East?" Kersta pressed.

"Just what you'd expect. Israel insists it's authentic; the Arabs naturally deny it and accuse Israel of making the whole thing up. So that's why we need your help with Voiceprints."

Kersta by now had brushed all doubts aside; this was exactly the kind of a job for him if he could be provided with what he needed. If this were possible, he was certain that Voiceprints could settle the issue.

He explained that he would need the tape that had been recorded in New York on a replay from Israel as well as another recording definitely known to be of Nasser's voice. He was assured that this would pose no problem but it was admitted that obtaining a sample of Hussein's known voice would be more difficult. Kersta replied that he believed just a tape of Nasser would be adequate.

"I'll undertake the job," Kersta finally announced, "but only on one important condition. I will do nothing without the approval of our American State Department. This is a very delicate situation."

On this note the conversation ended with the New Jersey scientist promising to call back as soon as he had received an answer from Washington.

The government approval that Kersta wanted was soon received. To his surprise, he got more—a State Department representative would fly to his laboratory to watch his work, if he did not object. Kersta was elated.

He called the New York office of the London paper to make final arrangements for the task he now was ready to undertake. In high excitement and anticipation, he awaited the arrival of the tape which was to be sent by car from New York to New Jersey together with a recording of a speech made by Nasser two years before and kept on file in the offices of CBS.

Less than three hours later Kersta had what he wanted, but the arrival of the two recordings marked only the beginning of what for him would probably be the most perplexing technical task he had ever undertaken. Actually it imposed difficulties far beyond his expectations.

Had the disputed conversation been in English his work would have been arduous enough, but it was in Arabic, which Kersta did not understand. First he must find a way to overcome this barrier.

He began by transforming the two tapes into Voiceprint pictures. This procedure he repeated over and over to avoid the slightest possibility of mechanical error. Though he did not understand any of the spoken words, he knew that words are only combinations of sounds. If he could not work with words as such, at least he could extract from them those sounds on which he could accurately base his comparisons.

For example, he took the sound of "ie," pronounced like the English word "eye," wondering if it might match the Voiceprints made from Nasser's known voice and of the talk attributed to him by the Israelis.

This, of course, was only a beginning, but he knew that he was on the right track. He had only to follow this intricate and laborious procedure with as many other sounds as he could extract from the Arabic—and there were many.

Customarily, working with English speech, Kersta often bases his comparative tests on ten commonly used words such as *me, you, to,* and the like. This time, working with a foreign tongue, he chose to compare a minimum of at least twenty-five familiar sounds taken from the Arabic tapes.

These he played over and over, converting them into Voiceprints and painstakingly comparing the patterns. It was a backbreaking task that consumed many hours. Night had fallen but Kersta was not yet ready to make a definite decision, though he already felt reasonably certain that one of the two taped voices in the dialogue was that of Nasser.

Meanwhile, in the offices of the London newspaper, editors waited tensely as they watched the clock, wondering when they might hear from the American scientist. Whatever his verdict, they would have a big and important news beat; either the Arabs had connived against the United States and Britain or Israel would be guilty of a daring plot to discredit her enemies. In either case it would be an exciting exposé that would be read and talked about by people not only in England but in other countries as well. For the newsmen it was a tantalizing wait, just as it was for those in the television studios.

In the New Jersey Voiceprint laboratories dawn already had broken when Kersta, tired but satisfied, turned to his colleagues and the government man close by and announced that his task was over: the voice was definitely that of Nasser.

While the study, of course, was confined to Nasser's voice, it was assumed that the other speaker must have been Hussein.

Minutes later Kersta was at his telephone, calling the New York office of the *London Telegraph*, which quickly relayed his conclusions to England. An enterprising newspaper and an equally resourceful television network had a most startling "scoop." Not long afterward the news was picked up by other publications, both in the United States and Europe.

As would be expected, spokesmen for the Arab countries belittled Kersta's findings, still accusing Israel of wanton trickery. However, as time passed, there were many who had followed the situation closely and believed that King Hussein, in a much later statement, had virtually acknowledged the authenticity of the conversation.

This was at a Washington press conference during Hussein's visit to the United States in which he met formally with the President and the State Department. When he met the press soon after these consultations, the Arab monarch was asked point-blank about the controversial dialogue. To this he replied in effect:

"That conversation was not accurately reported." He said no more, and many who heard his words later on radio and television were convinced that no doubt there was nothing more that he could say. And there the matter stands.

XXIII

Hughes Gets Equal Time

For sheer drama, billionaire Howard Hughes' long-distance telephone interview was probably without equal in recent years; in many other respects it was wholly unprecedented. The time was Friday, January 7, 1972.

Ironically, it was personally requested by the mysterious recluse, who had shunned newsmen and cameras for fifteen years, during which time he had remained out of public sight. The press regarded him as one of the most unapproachable men in America.

The talk, actually a conference between Hughes in the Bahamas and a panel in Los Angeles, lasted for two and a half hours, though Hughes stated that he had no desire to end it even then. He appeared most anxious to be heard.

He discussed a wide range of subjects, many of them intimate and extremely personal, but it was obvious that his principal purpose was to brand Clifford Irving's widely disputed biography of the celebrated financier an outright fake. All this, of course, was before Irving had confessed that the book was a hoax and had gone to prison to pay the penalty.

However, when the conversation was over, one baffling question of overwhelming importance remained: Was the speaker on the Caribbean island actually Hughes or a clever imitator? His seven interviewers, men who had talked with him at one time or another, answered with an emphatic yes. Irving stated just as emphatically that it was not.

To settle the question they turned to Voiceprints. And the answer, regarded as conclusive, came from pictures of the voice studied under the eyes of two men recognized as experts in the field. One of them was Lawrence G. Kersta.

Hughes' interviewers were seated in the Sheraton Universal Hotel in the Southern California city. They had assembled only two days after a top official of Hughes' vast industrial empire had sent word that such a conference was desired by the man who for years had dodged the press and any other form of publicity. The spokesman named the men wanted for the panel, for all of them had heard Hughes' voice and presumably would know the most personal questions to pose that would test the authenticity of the conference.

Hughes, by himself or in consultation with close associates, had set specific ground rules. Each panelist would be allowed two questions for purposes of identification so that the panelists might be assured that they were speaking to the man who, of his own volition, had emerged from years of seclusion. These definitely were to be in the nature of "trap questions."

The interviewers did their homework thoroughly as they prepared in advance for the unusual event. As soon as identification was disposed of, the actual press conference would proceed, each man asking whatever he chose.

There was only one other stipulation to which all agreed: there would be no publicity of any kind, either through the press or the networks, until the following Sunday. The reason for this request was not explained.

Seated around a semicircular table in Los Angeles were the panelists. One of them was Marvin Miles of *The Los Angeles Times*, to whose three-page detailed report of the conference, published in that newspaper, this writer is indebted for the facts. The others were Gladwin Hill of *The New York Times*, Wayne Thomas, *Chicago Tribune*; Gene Handsaker, Associated Press; Vernon Scott, United Press International; James Bacon for the Hearst newspapers; and Roy Neal of NBC News, serving as pool man for the major networks.

Each of these newsmen had his own microphone, through which he spoke directly.

At a given signal, Richard Hannah of the Hughes public relations corps dialed his principal's number at Paradise Island at Nassau and the voice presumed to be that of the billionaire came through clearly, amplified in the Los Angeles newsroom for the benefit of his listeners. At the other end television cameras had been set in motion.

The identifying questions began at once and the panelists soon nodded to each other, indicating their certainty that the voice they heard was actually that of Howard Hughes.

One of the first identifying questions concerned Hughes' early constellation transport and the problems involved in its cockpit design. Apparently he was pleased, for he moved into such a detailed response that a few wondered whether this was a trick to keep the conversation away from more pertinent subjects.

The interviewers, however, pressed still further to be positive that they actually were speaking to Hughes.

Miles came next with a tricky query recalling an inconsequential incident which had amused Hughes when it occurred. "At the time of your round-the-world trip in 1938," the newsman asked, "a superstitious woman placed a good luck charm on your airplane. What was it and where did she put it?"

Hughes hesitated for an instant. "Well," he said, "I want to be completely honest with you. I don't remember that one."

Miles followed quickly with his next and last identifying question, but before it was answered Hughes had recalled the first. A woman had stuck a wad of chewing gum on the tail of his plane.

The newsman's second inquiry, which was accurately answered, concerned Hughes' record-breaking flight in 1955 that ended disastrously in a forced landing in a field.

Other identifying questions of like nature brought quick responses. Twenty minutes had passed. The time now had come for the interview itself, and as Hughes undoubtedly had desired, it began with the issue of the controversial biography. He seemed eager to speak his mind.

The opening question was direct: "I'd like to ask about the so-called biography." The door now was wide open.

"So-called is a most important part of what you say," Hughes shot back without a moment's hesitation.

His interrogator was quick to follow. "Did you cooperate or know a man named Irving, who claims to have taped this biography with you?"

"This must go down in history," came the reply. "I only wish I was still in the movie business because I don't remember any script as wild or as stretching of the imagination as this yarn has turned out to be. I'm not talking about the biography itself because I have never read it. I don't know what's in it, but this episode is just so fantastic that it takes your imagination to believe that a thing like this could happen. I don't know him [Irving]. I never saw him. I have never even heard of him until a matter of days ago when this thing first came to my attention."

Here a panelist interrupted: "He claims you traveled around the Western Hemisphere with him over a period of several months ending late last year. Have you left your hotel there in the Bahamas in the last year?"

"Well, you are getting into a pretty touchy area," Hughes responded. "Let's say I haven't left the Bahamas and I certainly haven't seen Mr. Irving."

Another man inquired: "Do you feel this situation is merely the gullibility of a publishing firm, or is there something more sinister here, perhaps a carefully structured plot to discredit you?"

"My attorney thinks that it could be [a plan to discredit him]. I wouldn't attempt to pass judgment on McGraw-Hill's motives in this thing . . . deep-dyed or accidental gullibility; I have no way of judging that.

"I am so completely and utterly shocked that anything like this could have happened that, believe me, I don't know how to characterize this or diagnose it . . . it is so fantastic and so utterly beyond the bounds of anyone's imagination that I simply haven't any idea.

"Obviously the motive for Irving could be money," he

continued, "but certainly McGraw-Hill and Time-Life don't have to deal in fake manuscripts or that sort of thing in order to survive. They surely have a business that operates on a higher plane than that. I can say that assuming it's all an accident takes a whole lot of assuming."

Presumably Hughes was anxious to continue along this line, for he made no effort to digress into other areas. "Do you think it possible," he was asked, "there's a man going around representing himself as Howard Hughes and has duped this author?"

"No, that doesn't even seem possible to me," he replied quickly. "I mean it seems to me the author has ample motivation for doing this thing without being duped."

When the matter of the reported advance payments to both Hughes and Irving was introduced, the billionaire admitted with some apparent annoyance that his chief counsel had been unable to trace such funds despite claims that Hughes' signature appeared on a check. "I don't understand how such money as this could be passed through any normal channel without leaving a trail a mile wide and a bright pink," he asserted. "This money didn't come out of any of my bank accounts and it wasn't given to any charity with my knowledge or directions. So what happened to the money? In other words, if they paid me this money, as I understand they are claiming to have done, then where is it? I couldn't hide that amount of money without running into all sorts of difficulties with the Treasury Department."

At one point Hughes was queried about a reported telephone conversation between himself and Frank McCulloch, an old friend, the chief of the New York bureau of Time-Life News Service, concerning the book and publication of excerpts in *Life*. He spared no words in offering an explanation.

"Yes," he agreed. "I had one conversation with him and the nature of it was that we both agreed—at least I thought we both agreed—that it should not be done, that it couldn't possibly be valid. I thought we both agreed we were both going to scrap it and start talking about some kind of an accurate dissemination of news. In other words, I thought he agreed with me that this material you are describing should not be used and that it was not the type of thing that his people wanted to publish."

Discussion of the biography now was drawing to a close; the panelists were anxious to turn to even more intimate details of Hughes' current life and personal philosophy, but there remained one or two elements of the book subject to be cleared. He was asked whether he ever had considered writing his own life story and if the Irving book possibly might have been based on stolen tapes and other materials. In answer he stated that he had sold exclusive memoir rights to the Rosemont Corporation, his own concern, and that he could not conceive how Irving's book could have come from pilfered material.

"I have massive files, photographs, and other recorded material tracing my life from an early age," he went on. "I have just volumes and volumes and rooms full of photographic material, motion picture film, put away in vaults. I have rooms of this but the type of what Irving, I am told, has claimed to possess, I don't know where it could have come from. We have no indication that these vaults were burgled or the rooms in which any of the files were located have been entered or tampered with. . . . I just think this is a totally fantastic fiction."

No more was said about Irving or his book, but the panelists were to learn the answers to many other questions which they had been holding anxiously for years.

Hughes indicated that he was tired of living in seclusion in the Bahamas and planned to return to America, perhaps to Southern California or Las Vegas as soon as he could. On his return, he promised, he would gladly meet the press face to face. He disclosed, for probably the first time, that he contemplated philanthropy on a tremendous scale, that he planned to leave the bulk of his fabulous estate for medical research, hoping in this way to contribute to better health and living for his fellow men. And he indicated a keen concern for social welfare when one of his questioners asked whether he intended to dispose of any of his vast Las Vegas interests.

"I'll tell you what," he countered. "I have no intention of

selling anything that involves employment. In other words I have no intention of selling the active business you just mentioned—the hotels, Harold's Club in Reno or any in Nevada which account for the Hughes employment I have in Nevada."

Apparently he had been disturbed by rumors concerning ill health, with inferences of mental deterioration. Replying to such questions, he insisted that his health was as good as he had a right to expect.

"How the hell is anybody's health at sixty-six years of age," he exclaimed rather sharply. "I certainly don't feel like running around a track at UCLA and trying to break a record. I can tell you that. But my health is tolerable, that's certain, and probably better than I deserve. . . . I suppose I ought to be knocking on wood."

He was obviously most anxious to dispel rumors concerning idiosyncrasies in his personal appearance as well as the reasons for his isolated way of living.

Asked point-blank "Why do you live the way you do?" he replied reflectively:

"I don't really know—I sort of slid into it. I will tell you one thing. I am rapidly planning to come out of it. In other words, I am not going to continue being quite as reclusive, as you call it, as I have been, because I have just got to live a modified life in order not to be an oddity.

"It's a funny thing—it really is. In this world you can't just go about your business and live your life in what seems to you to be a normal way. This just doesn't seem possible. You apparently have to do certain things and follow a certain kind of conduct in order to satisfy people. So I'm getting ready to embark on a program of convincing the public that these extreme statements [reports about himself] are absurd."

Strangely, perhaps, he voiced a particular desire to squelch for all time rumors that his fingernails and toenails were eight inches long, that his beard reached to his chest, and that his hair fell down his back.

"This is inconceivable," he asserted with far more emphasis than he had shown in previous statements. "If I had toenails eight inches long I couldn't walk. If I had fingernails eight inches long I couldn't write my name." He added that he had worn a beard, a mustache and a Van Dyke for years. "As to hair to the middle of my back," he added, "where would I put it?"

One of the panelists was quick to follow this line of talk. "Why," he asked, "would somebody supposedly describe you that way?"

"In a malicious effort to discredit me and uphold those absurd statements that are being made," Hughes shot back. "This is all, obviously, part of a campaign to lend credence to the fairy tales that these people are trying, somehow, to support."

The closing question was appropriate for that moment: "Are you as happy as someone with two and a half billion dollars can be?"

Hughes paused before replying. "I'm not too—I'm not very happy, I'll tell you that," he confessed. "One of the primary reasons is because of some of the things we have been discussing here."

As already stated, news of the interview and its implications had barely reached the world by press, radio, and television, when the question of its authenticity was raised. Despite the certainty of the panelists that they had been talking to Hughes and no one else, Clifford Irving, personally and through his attorney, insisted that the voice was not that of the man in the Bahamas. It was inevitable that a controversy would develop quickly.

In anticipation, NBC-TV, which had handled the technical aspects of the long-distance conference, had prepared to meet the issue. Presumably, Kersta had been contacted in advance and informed that he would be called on to utilize Voiceprints to determine the authenticity of Hughes' voice.

Whether he was obliged to scurry about for a tape of Hughes' voice or had one in his files is not recorded. The important point is that he informed the network officials soon after the interview that he then had in his possession a recording of a speech made by the seclusive financier during his testimony before a subcommittee of the United States Senate some years before.

Kersta did have one question to ask, though he knew that it was superfluous, "I'm assuming," he told the network people, "that you have ample tapes of the voice that you believe has come from Hughes."

"Plenty of it," he was informed. He directed that it be sent to him immediately by airmail and special delivery.

No time was lost in meeting the request and Kersta's reply was anxiously awaited.

In the meantime, however, a new complication entered the already confused situation. In New York officials of the concern undertaking publication of Irving's book brushed aside all that had been said against the authenticity of the biography. Not only that, but they announced formally that publication would take place as planned on March 27. A formal statement said in part:

"It is alleged that Howard Hughes made a telephone call Friday repudiating this material and the man who worked on it with him, Clifford Irving."

This was read over the telephone to Hughes and he was quick to respond: "It looks as if we'll have to do it the hard way. It is becoming apparent that it may never be settled anywhere other than in court."

Irving himself stepped into the controversy, amplifying his earlier statement that he did not believe that Hughes actually had done the talking. He insisted that the voice heard over telephone and television from the Bahamas was "much too vigorous" and much too deep. "For anyone who hasn't talked to him for twenty-five years it was an excellent forgery," Irving declared.

Tension and curiosity increased. Would the dispute reach its climax in one of the strangest and most sensational courtroom battles over the authorship of a book, or would Kersta's Voiceprints provide a final and indisputable answer? People wondered as they awaited word from the scientist in New Jersey.

Kersta took a few days to respond because he was staking his reputation on his findings and was unwilling to hasten his technical tests to satisfy the curiosity of an anxious public. The tape recordings, of course, had been converted into spectograms and Kersta spent long hours in his laboratory comparing the voice pictures line for line.

When he had finished he had a definite answer for the network that had engaged him for the delicate, intricate, scientific task.

He reported with complete assurance that the voice heard over the telephone from Nassau was indeed that of Howard Hughes and of no one else. "The matches we got were excellent," he explained. "We are as near to one hundred percent positive as a scientist would ever allow himself to be."

Science now had spoken through the man widely recognized as the Voiceprint "inventor," but others interested in the issue turned to one more expert in the field, Dr. Peter Ladefoged, a professor of phonetics at the University of California in Los Angeles, whose opinion, it was agreed, would be of value, especially if he agreed with the Kersta conclusions.

There was a very special reason why they wanted Dr. Ladefoged's judgment. In the early days of Voiceprint experiments he had been extremely critical of Kersta's methods, insisting that the process required infinitely more testing and development before it could be accepted as a worthwhile tool in scientific crime detection. After advances had been made in the process, however, and at the conclusion of the two-year Tosi studies, he changed his mind and said he was willing to accept Voiceprints, though they still required further improvements. In fact, he had been called a number of times as a witness in cases involving spectograms and had been accepted as an expert.

After spending hours in his laboratory with a spectrograph, measuring pitch, tone, volume and other elements of the voices, he announced that "I'm reasonably certain that those two recordings are of the same voice.

"Even considering the age difference . . . it is difficult to believe that this could be two different voices."

In his mention of age differences, he was referring to the fact that Hughes was thirty-three years of age when he made the recording used by the Los Angeles professor for comparison.

Voiceprints, studied and interpreted by two scientists, had authenticated the voice as that of Howard Hughes. And if still further verification were needed, it obviously came from Clifford Irving himself when he confessed that the biography in fact was a hoax.

XXIV

A Matter
of Sounds

Over the radio came the first shocking news of an appalling plane disaster.

Details were meager. Only minutes before, a few early risers in the little town of Danville on the easterly side of San Francisco Bay had looked on in horror as a huge airliner suddenly plummeted in a power dive out of the skies, crashing at terrific speed into a hillside. Seconds later it had become a seething, fiery mass. Obviously all on board had perished.

Hourly bulletins broadcast throughout the morning added to the shock of the earlier news. The crash had been one of the worst in recent years. Its cause was a mystery that was to grow in proportions as days passed.

The ill-fated passenger carrier had been a two-engined Fairchild turbo-jet operated by Pacific Airlines. It was flying from Reno to San Francisco International Airport carrying forty-one passengers and a crew of three.

The tragedy had occurred shortly before seven o'clock on a clear, sunny Thursday morning, May 7, 1964. Minutes later all would have landed safely. No turbulence in the upper air had been reported; there was no apparent reason for what had occurred.

The first police and deputy sheriffs to reach the scene turned their attention to the scant possibility of survivors. As they quickly looked about, however, it was obvious that all on board had met horrible deaths. Fragments of the pitifully torn forty-four bodies were strewn over a wide area—a hand here, a leg there. Identification, it was apparent, could be made only with the aid of fingerprints. Nor was there any section of the plane intact; it had been reduced to pieces of twisted metal, shredded fabrics, and other debris. The engines had been torn apart as if by giant hands; small sections were scattered about, some of them buried deep in the ground by the terrific force of the impact.

While airline officials were hastening to the scene, local authorities busied themselves interviewing David Silva, a nearby rancher, and the few others who had actually seen the plane in its downward plunge. "I was looking up from my barnyard," Silva related, "when I saw this thing falling out of the sky. Then came the crash, seconds later. God only knows how such a thing could have happened on a clear day like this."

Willing hands moved quickly about, undertaking the grim task of gathering fragments of bodies, dropping them into bags, and moving them to an emergency morgue set up in Danville. Others turned their attention to picking up pieces of wreckage and depositing them in what became huge heaps dumped on a campsite in the Santa Rita Rehabilitation Center. It was a task that would consume many weeks, with more than a thousand fragments finally landing in the enormous piles.

News of the wreck had already reached Washington and word came quickly that experts from the FBI, the Civil Aeronautics Board, and other agencies were starting west at once, expecting to arrive before night.

They were anxiously awaited by the airline officials who surveyed the scene in amazement, unable to comprehend the reason for the disaster. Was it due to some mechanical defect or to some inexplicable human error by the pilots? They could only wonder as they recalled the outstanding record of the top man at the controls, Captain Ernest A. Clark, a veteran at fifty-two, who had been flying for thirty-five years. He had started his career by building his own plane, later became a commercial flying instructor, and finally served in the air force as a captain, piloting huge transport planes. He was regarded as one of the most competent men in the company's employ.

Even as speculation continued, Pacific Airlines executives gave little if any thought to the remote possibility of sabotage. Any such attempt, even if hatched in the air, could have been handled by Clark, they said, especially with the assistance of his copilot, Ray E. Andress, a judo expert and son of an FBI agent. Later developments, however, were to prove them wrong.

One by one government officials began arriving from Washington. By morning a small army of investigators had assembled and organized themselves into nine teams, each assigned to a specific phase of the inquiry. To Jack Carroll, a long-experienced CAB specialist in mysteries of this kind, had gone the task of assembling a mock-up, a huge frame replica of the aircraft into which would be fitted with meticulous care and expert knowledge every fragment of the plane that could be recovered. He also would try to re-create the flight itself.

Hours later, Carroll eyed the dummy structure and realized that he was actually working with a giant jigsaw puzzle that might never be completed. Whether it would ever tell a story was a matter of conjecture.

For assistance he had called in a corps of cartographers from the U.S. Coast and Geodetic Survey, who began drawing maps of the hillside and surrounding region, hoping that these might help in determining the areas where the greatest amount of wreckage would be found.

Others turned to hunting for charred remnants of luggage that might possibly provide a clue. The task of attempting to identify the victims from the scant fragments of flesh and bones was left to local men, who began their work under the direction of experts. Many of the passengers were believed to be Bay Area people who had gone to Reno for a few days of fun in the gambling casinos.

While all of this was going on as the first stage of the investigation, a curious, puzzling element in the mystery was being studied by the government's specialists in radio communication. It concerned the last message ever to come from the unfortunate plane to the control tower at Oakland airport.

Moments before the crash, operators there had listened to and recorded these words from Captain Clark:

"Oakland flight control. This is Pacific 773-5000," which meant that he was flying at an altitude of 5,000 feet, well above the low hills on the east side of San Francisco Bay.

"Keep that altitude," came the reply, with the added note that "your transmitter is garbled."

"Roger!" Clark had responded. "How do you read now?"

"It still has the same space sounds like over-modulation," and the man in the tower waited for an answer that never came. Instead he listened to crackling, garbled sounds, all of them incomprehensible—and then only silence. A second later came the crash.

The garbled message probably was the key to the mystery. What had the skipper been trying to say? Was it something important that could not be heard because of transmitter trouble? Or had the airliner started its fatal plunge before the captain could explain his difficulties? A dead pilot held the answer.

Some theorized that the mock-up, when completed, might disclose a mechanical failure. Others, more skeptical, feared that the tragic end of the flight would become just another of the many unsolved mysteries of air fatalities. The real answer was furthest from their minds.

Days and nights of feverish work by the nine well-functioning teams passed without a clue to the cause of the disaster. Piece after piece was added to the mock-up, but thousands more were missing. However, progress was being made in identifying the victims. A week after the crash the names of thirty-four adults and two children had been ascertained, mostly by fingerprint comparisons.

Victims included the usual assortment of travelers. There had been the Rev. Lon Eakes, eighty-eight years of age, the oldest living alumnus of Emory University in Georgia, on his way to a reunion in Atlanta. Among others was twenty-four-year-old Polly Johnson, a gospel singer en route to the start of a concert tour, and George Butler, father of seven. Police Inspector George Lacau of San Francisco and his wife, Betty, were returning home. A number had come from other Northern California communities. The stewardess, pretty thirty-year-old Margaret Schafer, was the mother of a daughter of eleven.

In honor of these victims and those who perhaps never would be identified, a grim memorial service was held by the townsfolk of Danville assembled near the hillside where most of the wreckage had fallen. It took place two days after the crash, a touching tribute by the country people shocked by the tragedy at their doorstep.

The first hopeful turn in the frustrating investigation occurred one night during one of the many conferences held by the officials in charge. It was a suggestion by an expert for the FAA, now known as the National Transportation Safety Board. He was referring, as he had before, to the garbled end of the last radio call from the plane, the message that had proved wholly unintelligible.

"I've had a feeling from the start," he reasoned slowly, "that if only we could get something out of the crackles in that last message we'd have a lead that—"

"But we've listened to that tape dozens of times," one man interrupted. "There isn't even a syllable to give us an inkling of what it means."

"Then why shouldn't we let that man Kersta in New Jersey take a try at it with his Voiceprints?" the other proposed. "If he can't do anything, and I doubt if he can, we won't be any worse off than we are now."

More discussion followed until it was finally decided to reach Kersta by telephone to at least discuss the problem.

Kersta listened as the situation was related, occasionally interrupting before he would venture an answer. "Sounds like a pretty difficult matter," he said at last, "something I've never been asked to do before. But I'm willing to try, if you want me to."

He asked that the tape from the tower be sent to him together with a recording of Captain Clark's voice as it had been taped many times before. Kersta knew, of course, that federal regulations require that all messages from moving planes to airport towers be recorded on tape.

The scientist had still another request. "Must have been a co-pilot in that plane," he said. "I'll need a tape of his voice, too."

They told him that Ray Andress had sat beside Clark at the control. Yes, Andress's voice had been taped frequently at the Oakland tower. That recording would be sent along with the other, and in a sense, Kersta's task would be to "fingerprint" the crackling sounds in the tape that no one could understand.

In his New Jersey laboratory Kersta first played the garbled tape and his face fell. He heard only sounds so muffled and blurred that not even the semblance of a syllable was audible. To make matters worse, the tape crackled with engine sounds and high-pitched electrical squeaks.

At once Kersta realized that he faced a task that never had confronted him before and he feared that it was insurmountable. Yet here was a new kind of challenge and he was known to delight in tackling the seemingly impossible. Perhaps he could find some way to translate strange, unintelligible sounds into meaningful words. At all events he wanted to try, but first he must eliminate the static and rumbling sounds of the engine.

To accomplish this there was the possible danger of excluding words as well as static. It was a danger that somehow he must avoid.

Using an electronic filter of his own design, he devoted himself to the effort to eliminate interference. This took days to accomplish, but at last he detected something that sounded like a human voice. Of this he made spectograms, comparing them, faint as they were, with patterns from the tapes of the two pilots' voices. It appeared possible that the voice was that of the co-pilot, but this was only a supposition.

By now he was convinced that he must proceed with sounds only, with those that appeared to have come from a human being. Working with one sound after another, he used his spectograph until he had many hundred graphs of every one. These he compared and studied with meticulous care, spending hour after hour in that process alone.

Still there remained the disturbing thought that he might be misinterpreting what he heard. There was only one way to guard against such error. He would himself utter the sounds as he believed he had heard them, then check them against those coming actually from the tape.

At last he thought that he had detected a complete word—"stock"—but he was far from certain. He tried again; perhaps it might be "skit," but the spectogram told him that he was wrong again.

Then he uttered another word—"skip"—and changed it into a spectrogram, comparing it hopefully with his graph of the same word as it had come from the recording. Now Kersta's face lighted for the first time; the patterns seemed to match.

Pursuing this course with infinite patience, he finally produced the word "skipper," and he knew now that at last he was on the right track; that his long labors were producing some result.

The next move was to try by the same process to find the second word, pronouncing in his own voice what it seemed to be and checking it against the recorded sound. Perhaps it was "stop," but he knew that this must be wrong.

He repeated the procedure over and over. A full day passed before he had it. The word was "shot" and it made sense.

After nearly a full week of the same painstaking, tenacious effort he had deciphered the entire garbled tape into these shocking words, obviously uttered by Andress:

"Skipper's shot . . . we've been shot . . . tryin' ta help."

Further tests convinced him that the words had been spoken by the co-pilot.

Kersta had accomplished what once had been regarded as impossible. Now the curtain was rising on the second act of this tragic drama, which one FBI man chose to call "one of the most astounding air tragedies in the nation's history."

The inquiry in California suddenly took on new directions.

"If the pilot was shot and killed in flight," the probers reasoned, "we must find somewhere a weapon or a fragment of one." Already, on a remote chance, they had been searching for such evidence but nothing of the kind had been found.

J. Edgar Hoover, who had interested himself personally in the mystery, now directed his agents at the crash site to spare no effort in finding some remnant of a gun.

The search went on; days slipped by. Then one morning one of the investigators suddenly came upon what everyone had been looking for—a revolver with two discharged shells, buried in the dust under a clump of shrubbery nearly a mile from the scene of the crash. It was sent immediately by air to FBI headquarters in Washington, where experts, tracing its number, found that it was registered in the name of William High of Los Angeles.

In the southern city, High was located and a new name came into the case when High explained that he had sold his Smith & Wesson revolver to an acquaintance named Frank Gonzales, a twenty-seven-year-old soldier of fortune who lived and worked in San Francisco. "And I'd sure like to get my hands on him now," High told the FBI man. "He gave me a hundred-and-thirty-dollar check for the gun and his check bounced."

Gonzales's name was on the passenger list of the lost plane.

Soon the drama was beginning to unfold as investigators turned their attention to Gonzales, tracing his recent movements and probing into his background. A strange and bizarre story of his life came to light as agents pressed their inquiries among those who had known the man in San Francisco and in Reno.

Gonzales, they learned, was a native of the Philippines, a well-known handsome and debonair athlete, whose nickname was "Kiko." Only a few years before he had competed in the Olympic Games on a Filipino team.

He was a yachtsman, often sailing with the elite. He could also be found serving the elite in exclusive dining places where he sometimes worked as a waiter. Recently he had been employed as a shipping clerk in a San Francisco department store. He was somewhat of a mystery.

A week before the crash he had gone to Reno to try his luck at the gambling tables and had lost heavily. Several who had met him in the casinos related an ironic circumstance. He had told them of his visit to a palmist who, he said, looked at his hand

and predicted that he was destined to die on Thursday morning, May 7, the day of the disaster. Another odd detail came from an attendant at a dice table where Gonzales had been losing steadily. "Keep trying," an onlooker had told him consolingly, "your luck is bound to change." But the player merely shrugged his shoulders and laughed as he remarked that "after tomorrow it won't make any difference if I win or lose."

Others had equally significant things to tell, further indicating that Gonzales had carefully planned his deed well in advance. One had observed a revolver in Gonzales's pocket while he was gambling; another had watched him loading a handgun in an airport restroom shortly before takeoff.

These facts and others as they came to light bolstered the conclusions of a panel of FBI and CAB men concerned with reconstructing the crime. In an unexpected way they already had learned exactly where Gonzales had been seated during the flight. That information, dovetailing perfectly with their theory, had come from an airport attendant to whom "Kiko" had spoken briefly after stepping from the plane to spend a few parting moments on the ground. To this person he had remarked casually that he had picked "a nice front seat nearest to the pilot."

This information thoroughly confirmed the theory of those reconstructing the case. They had found a piece of tubing that they identified as coming from the upper corner of the backrest frame of the pilot's seat. It bore the indentation of a bullet.

The little piece of tubing, closely studied in the FBI laboratory in Washington, attracted the special attention of Hoover, who made this comment:

"This bullet indentation is so positioned that it would have been directly in line of fire between the pilot and anyone standing in the aisleway between and slightly to the rear of the pilot and co-pilot."

Should anyone have questioned Gonzales's presence in the plane, the FBI was ready to explain that a lone finger found in the wreckage area had been positively identified by fingerprints as his.

The CAB, soon afterward, announced that it had closed its

investigation, completely satisfied that murder had been committed in midair.

In the opinion of investigators, Gonzales probably had ended his own life immediately after shooting the pilots, for a small piece of human hand, matching his fingerprints, was found later and showed definite evidence of a bullet wound.

The authorities were convinced that Gonzales, acting on some frenzied impulse, had planned his every move well in advance, even to maneuvering his way to the most forward seat from which the pilots would be easy targets. They reasoned that after shooting Captain Clark he had turned his gun on Andress, the co-pilot, while the latter, in desperation, was attempting to broadcast further details to the control tower. He little thought that the flyer's last words, garbled in excitement and by static, would betray the atrocious deed.

The tragedy, however, had its echoes in the courts for many months. Suit after suit was filed, some by relatives of the victims against the airline, others against an insurance company with whom Gonzales had taken an airport policy for a large sum shortly before his departure. This naturally led to speculation that Gonzales's motive was to provide insurance money for at least some of his survivors.

Litigation was based on two specific claims. Some contended that the pilots' compartment should have been locked; others that Gonzales himself should have been closely watched on the presumption that he probably had been acting strangely with an apparent show of nerves.

One passenger's widow was awarded $280,000. A suit against an insurance company for $105,000, brought by Gonzales's father, Joaquin, and his estranged wife, Patricia, was dismissed because of a suicide clause in the policy. Some of the other actions were settled out of court.

What really drove Gonzales to his diabolical act remains a mystery that even Voiceprints cannot solve.

XXV

Tomorrow—
and Afterward

What does the future hold for Voiceprints?

Will they win increasing acceptance in the crime laboratory? If so, can they also become vitally important factors in medicine, industry, mechanics, and business administration, as some supporters of the Kersta method believe?

Opinions differ, especially concerning the broadening use of Voiceprints in other fields than crime. Yet there are those who assert that the technique has potentials far beyond criminal justice, just as fingerprints are being used today in areas unthought of at the time of their original acceptance.

Many point to the fact that imagination as well as technical progress often opens up new channels and leads to new directions. Some even refer significantly to the curious influence which the fanciful writings of novelists have had on real-life innovations. For example, they cite Mark Twain's fictional prediction that fingerprints would win popular acceptance—a forecast made in 1894, six years before the method was adopted by Scotland Yard. His imaginative story "Pudd'n head Wilson" is credited with having focused serious attention in America on a technique that many ridiculed at the time.

And while Lawrence Kersta in New Jersey was still trying to find a positive way of putting Voiceprints to useful purpose, a celebrated writer in Russia, Alexander L. Solzhenitsyn, the Nobel Prize-winner exiled by Russia, devoted a chapter to

Voiceprints in his book *The First Circle*. With incredible foresight the novelist detailed the spectrogram process as if it were a recognized technique in everyday use.

Though major attention has centered on the potentials of Voiceprints in criminalistics, their possible use in medicine has provoked serious speculation. Many have listened with tongue in cheek to the claims of Dr. Oscar Tosi of Michigan State University that the sound spectrograph could become an important aid to physicians; that it could detect physical defects through the recorded sounds they emitted.

"Can this be possible?" some have asked almost incredulously. "Tosi isn't even a medical doctor."

But now, as recently as February, 1974, an affirmative answer has come. In San Francisco two staff psychiatrists at Langley Porter Neuropsychiatric Institute of the University of California have announced their success in diagnosing birth defects in babies by studying their cries through the spectograph —in other words by Voiceprints.

These medics, Drs. Peter F. Ostwald and Philip Peltman, have reported their work in an article published in *Scientific America*. "We have been able," they have written, "to identify the distress cry of infants but also the presence of abnormalities and diseases by the characteristic cry of the affected infants. Spectographic analysis of infant cries has a definite value for the diagnosis of a number of infections and developmental conditions."

They assert that one apparently normal newborn infant, through its cry, was found to have a disabling birth defect—no cerebral cortex, or top part of the brain.

The sound spectograph which produces Voiceprints was used to "break up" the sounds of the child's cries into different frequencies and rates of vibrations per second. This was accomplished, of course, by minute study of the well-lined spectograms made from tape recordings of the cries.

Despite this surprising report of the medical men, it is to the field of criminalistics and law that most supporters of Voiceprints look for an expanding use of the technique. They eagerly anticipate the day when files of police departments will be crammed with voice recordings of new and old offenders, complementing the tremendous bank of fingerprints maintained by authorities everywhere—hundreds of millions in FBI headquarters in Washington alone.

Speculation on the potential value of such Voiceprint files continues. Some point to celebrated kidnappings of recent years, mysteries in which an unidentified person calls over the telephone or sends his victim's family a tape-recorded message demanding ransom.

In such cases the voice of the extortioner could be checked almost immediately with the filed spectograms of known offenders then at large and put to quick and valuable use, as effectively as clues are obtained through fingerprints.

Others with perhaps even greater foresight look into still different directions. Knowing of significant results obtained by the FBI through its vast fingerprint files of law-abiding civilians, gathered from civil service and other personnel lists, they argue that a huge bank of Voiceprints of men and women in civilian life would be valuable in cases of amnesia victims who have completely forgotten their identity.

And there are also those who believe that Voiceprints could make important contributions in such national affairs as the Watergate scandal. They recall the hoax perpetrated by an unidentified imposter who, posing as Treasury Secretary George Shultz, informed Senator Sam Ervin that President Nixon had agreed to surrender all tapes of White House conversations. Had the spurious telephone call been recorded, they say, it could have been compared with Voiceprints of the culprit had he been apprehended. In this instance, of course, he was never found.

To return to Dr. Tosi and his confidence in other Voiceprint potentials, he further suggests that sounds produced by automobile motors could be recorded to facilitate detection of mechanical troubles. In other words, a motorist encountering engine difficulties could merely drive into a shop with spectographic equipment and learn within minutes the exact source of trouble.

An equally optimistic outlook on future uses of Voiceprints in crime detection is presented in a recent volume, *Voice*

Identification Research, published by the United States Department of Justice through its Law Enforcement Assistance Administration. With lengthy dissertations on the subject by both Department of Audiology and Speech Science of Michigan State University and the Sensory Sciences Research Center of Stanford Research Center in California, it presents this significant conclusion written at the Michigan institution:

"There are other research projects that should be instituted to extend the effectiveness of the voice spectograph in criminal investigation. This would include experimentation with the identification of disguised voices and non-contemporary recordings. However, this should not deter its use by forensic laboratories or interfere with efforts to present voice identification testimony in court. In this respect, voice identification is no different than other forensic sciences in that there are always new questions to be answered. . . .

"The possibility of using the spectograph to identify sounds other than the human voice should not be overlooked. As an example, let us imagine that an anonymous bomb threat is received and recorded. The sound of a motor can be distinguished as part of the background noise. If the motor noise, through sound spectography, can be identified as to type, it might help investigators locate the source of the call. Again let us imagine that a woman calls the police and says that she is about to be shot. An explosive sound ends the conversation. The sound spectograph in this case may be effective in identifying the explosive noise as a firearm, perhaps a rifle rather than a pistol, and of large caliber.

"As time passes, investigators and examiners alike will discover new applications of the sound spectograph as it relates to criminal investigations. It remains now for more agencies and individuals to become involved in developing expertise and gaining experience in order that this relatively new technique can reach its full potential for solving crime."

Michigan State University, however, is not the only institution still deeply involved in such research. At Stanford Research Center, Michael H. L. Hecker and Fausto Poza, specialists in audiology, devote much of their time to a continuing study of Voiceprints, delving into the accuracy of the process and its potentials.

However, officials at Interpol, the International Criminal Police Organization, with headquarters at St. Cloud, a Paris suburb, inform this writer that most European law-enforcement departments, with the exception of Switzerland, view Voiceprints with decided skepticism.

Interpol's expansive library contains many articles written in the United States and abroad on the subject. In a Paris publication, the writer, Christian Sacase, states that specialists in that country take a dubious view of Voiceprints. Dr. Alfred Tomatis is quoted as saying that the method still remains in the "domain of the laboratory," while Professor Bernard Vallancien, director of L'Institut Français de la Voix, questions the accuracy of voice comparisons.

While Scotland Yard does not use the method at the present time, an article in the Interpol archives describes the effective application of Voiceprints in England in 1967. This occurred in a Winchester Magistrates Court when spectograph pictures of a male voice were used to identify a speaker as the person who had made malicious telephone calls to attendants at a fire station. A tape recording of the anonymous voice was played in court and compared with one made by the accused.

To pass expert judgment on the claimed similarity of voices, the prosecution had summoned David Ellis, a lecturer in English at Leeds University, who had for close to two decades studied speech and phonetics.

Ellis listened to the playoff and studied the spectograms before testifying. "There is a very considerable degree of correspondency," he declared. "My opinion is that the voices are the same."

The defendant was found guilty and fined.

Japan, in recent years, has taken a serious interest in voice comparisons and their place in criminal work. The subject is treated in a lengthy article published by Interpol. The writer is Seiki Miyoshi, professor of phonetics at Kyoto.

Since 1965 Miyoshi has concerned himself with tests to determine the relations between facial bones and vocal sounds.

He cites a study of identical twins who resembled each other so closely that even relatives were hard put to tell them apart. The physical similarity extended even to their voices.

His interest is largely centered on hard-palate bone patterns, which he says "are more reliable than fingerprints or Voiceprints because they cannot be changed artifically." Results of his extensive research in this unique field received much attention at the Second World Congress of Phoneticians in Tokyo in 1965.

In a more realistic vein, perhaps, was a report published in June, 1973, by the New York *Post* stating that the FBI, acting for the CIA, had requested Radio WMCA, a New York "call in" station, to record all incoming conversations critical of the President and his associates.

A spokesman for that station disclaimed such a broad demand but explained that all conversations are recorded on tape. He also stated that on one occasion WMCA had received a request from the CIA for a recording of a specific conversation of a threatening nature against the administration.

No doubt differences of opinion and conflicting court decisions on the value and use of Voiceprints will continue for many years. Such, apparently, has been the way of all pioneering into new fields of science.

In this case, who can foretell the future? Only trial and time will provide the answer.

INDEX